ANNALS OF AN ANGUS PARISH.
[AUCHTERHOUSE]

ANNALS OF AN ANGUS PARISH. [AUCHTERHOUSE]

Inglis, W. Mason

www.General-Books.net

Publication Data:

Title: Annals of an Angus Parish. [auchterhouse]
Author: Inglis, W. Mason
Publisher: Dundee, Leng
Publication date: 1888
Subjects: Auchterhouse (England : Parish)

How We Made This Book for You
We made this book exclusively for you using patented Print on Demand technology.
First we scanned the original rare book using a robot which automatically flipped and photographed each page.
We automated the typing, proof reading and design of this book using Optical Character Recognition (OCR) software on the scanned copy. That let us keep your cost as low as possible.
If a book is very old, worn and the type is faded, this can result in typos or missing text. This is also why our books don't have illustrations; the OCR software can't distinguish between an illustration and a smudge.
We understand how annoying typos, missing text or illustrations, foot notes in the text or an index that doesn't work, can be. That's why we provide a free digital copy of most books exactly as they were originally published. Simply go to our website (www.general-books.net) to check availability. And we provide a free trial membership in our book club so you can get free copies of other editions or related books.
OCR is not a perfect solution but we feel it's more important to make books available for a low price than not at all. So we warn readers on our website and in the descriptions we provide to book sellers that our books don't have illustrations and may have typos or missing text. We also provide excerpts from each book to book sellers and on our website so you can preview the quality of the book before buying it.
If you would prefer that we manually type, proof read and design your book so that it's perfect, simply contact us for the cost. We would be happy to do as much work as you would be like to pay for.

Limit of Liability/Disclaimer of Warranty:
The publisher and author make no representations or warranties with respect to the accuracy or completeness of the book. The advice and strategies in the book may not be suitable for your situation. You should consult with a professional where appropriate. The publisher is not liable for any damages resulting from the book.
Please keep in mind that the book was written long ago; the information is not current. Furthermore, there may be typos, missing text or illustration and explained above.

1

ANNALS OF AN ANGUS PARISH.
[AUCHTERHOUSE]

PREFACE.

SOME years ago (1881) the writer of the following Notes upon an old Angus Parish delivered several lectures upon the past history of the parish of Auchterhouse copious extracts from which appeared at the time in the Dundee press. At the request of many of the parishioners and others to whom they proved somewhat interesting, the writer has consented to their publication in extenso. They are the result of careful and laborious reading and research into many quaint and interesting departments of historical and ecclesiastical literature. To those of antiquarian tastes they may probably possess more than a merely local interest.

THE Parish of Aucliterhouse may have derived its name from Achter, the high ground on which the church stands; or from Achadh Torr, the house with the tower in the field. According to modern authorities the name signifies the kirk on the height. In old documents the name appears as Auchtirhous, Ochtirhous, Ouchterhous, Owchtirous, Ochirhous, Uchterhous, Uchtirhouse, Uchtirhous, Utherhous.

The parish lies in the south-west corner of Forfarshire, and is bounded on the south by Liff; west and south-west by Lundie and Fowlis; north-west by Newtyle; north and north-east by Glands; east by Tealing; south-east by Mains and Strath-martine. The figure of the parish is a triangle, its base being the Vale of the Dighty, while the Hill of Aucliterhouse or White Top of Sidlaw forms the apex.

The oldest family of historic interest associated with the parish is that of Earnsay, well known in early Scottish history as the Eamsays of Ochterhous, from a branch of which the present family of Dalhousie is descended. The family was unquestionably one of considerable antiquity and distinction, for Boece states that when the supporters of Edgar Atheling were outlawed by William the Conqueror, and sought a retreat in Scotland, among the distinguished families who received grants of land from Malcolm was that of Eamsay. Sir George Mackenzie also designates it a very ancient and honourable family, which from its antiquity possessed the privilege of bearing the Eagle, then reckoned a mark of illustrious ancestry. Simundus de Eamesie is witness to a charter in the reign of King David I. (1140), and the name of William de Eamesie frequently appears in the charters of William the Lion. William of Hwuchtyruus, who was also a Eamsay, held the position of Sheriff of Angus in 1245. This important office of High Sheriff of Angus was of an hereditary character, and was for a lengthened period held by the proprietors of the lands of Ochterhous.

In the year 1296, Edward I., King of England, bent upon the subjugation of Scotland, advanced from England with thirty thousand infantry and five thousand mounted men-at-arms, and seized the important town and stronghold of Berwick. Erom that town his advance through Scotland seems to have been one continued triumphal march. Eesistance to such a force was impossible on the part of a people whose natural leaders the nobility had with great cowardice submitted to the English rule and dictation.

On his return to Berwick, on the 22nd August 1296, all the great territorial potentates, barons, knights, and leading churchmen of Scotland presented themselves to take the oath of allegiance. On this list of the Scottish nobility, which is still preserved in the English archives, appears the name of Thomas de Eamsay, Baron of the lands of Ochterhouse. The submission of so many nobles and prelates appears to have been accomplished quite as much by liberal bribes and grants of lands as by force of arms. It must also be borne in mind that many of the Scottish nobles were practically foreigners Anglo-Normans and Anglo-Saxons whose only attachment to their adopted country consisted in the fact that they were the owners of great tracts of its soil. Whilst these nobles seem to have accepted the

English domination with perfect equanimity, and in too many cases with great satisfaction, it was differently viewed, however, by the generality of the Scottish people. On their part, the greatest possible resentment was exhibited towards the brutality of the English usurpers and oppressors, and it soon became impossible for them longer to tolerate such abject national humiliation and degradation. Outbreaks against Southern violence and tyranny became frequent amongst the hardy, stalwart peasantry, in whom the spirit of pure patriotism still remained unsubdued. Nothing, however, of any significance Avas achieved by them in asserting their rights and regaining their liberties, owing to the lack of leaders, until Wallace became the head of the national movement. Then the Scots showed that under competent leadership they were a fierce and high-spirited people. Putting himself at the head of a meagre but resolute band of patriots, Wallace was not long in proving to the Southrons that Scotland was not to be so easily subjugated and reduced to a position of utter servility under England. Possessing great physical strength and courage of the highest order, animated by the purest and most disinterested motives, ever ready personally to brave every hardship and sacrifice all that he held most dear for liberty, his valour, enthusiasm, youthful ardour, and pure patriotism, had a marvellous effect upon all true Scots who came in contact with 'him.

When we consider the might of England, her wealth, her vast resources, the splendid character of her chivalry, the thoroughness with which the Plantagenets achieved the objects of their ambition, it seemed folly to embark in such an enterprise, and simply an idle dream to entertain thoughts of national independence. Put it was no phantasy of over-confident youth, it was no mad freak destined to vanish away and terminate in disaster; it was the beginning of a protracted struggle, which culminated in the complete triumph, by force of arms, of Scottish manhood,. and the future undeniable recognition of the national title and claim for independence.

The successes of Wallace and Douglas aroused the energies of others, and summoned a few members of the old nobility to share in the national struggle. Conspicuous among them was Sir John Ramsay of Ochterhous. The bold exploits of the great patriot throughout the West of Scotland appear to have kindled his patriotism, and led him fearlessly into the noble, yet perilous, enterprise of aiding in the liberation of his native land. Sir John Ramsay first took up arms against the English in the district of Strathearn, where with a small but resolute body of men he continued persistently to harass and attack the enemy. His accession to the side of Wallace brought about the immediate confiscation of his estates, and reduced him to great privation. Ramsay appears to have joined Wallace when he had withdrawn his forces, after many stirring adventures amid the Western wilds, to Ardchattan on the banks of Loch Etive. The incident is thus recorded by Henry the Minstrel:

"Mony trew Scot to Wallace couth persew; At Archatan fra feill strenthis thai drew. A gud knycht come, and with him men sexte; He had beyn oft in mony Strang jeperte With Inglissmen, and sonyeid nocht adeill. Ay fra thar faith he fendyt him full weill; Kepyt him fre, thocht king Eduuard had suorne; Schir Jhon Ramsay, that rychtwyss ayr was borne Off Ouchterhous, and othir landis was lord, And schirreff als, as my buk will record; Off nobill blud, and alss haill ancestre; Contenyt weill with worthi chewalre. In till Straithern that lang tyme he had beyne, At gret debait agaynys his enemyss keyne; Rycht wichtly wan his lewing in to wer; Till him and his Sotheroun did mekill der; Weill eschewit, and suffer 't gret distress. Wallace off him rycht full gud comford hais: For weill he coud do gret harmyng till his fais. In wer he was rycht mekill for to prys; Eesy and trew, baith sobyr, wicht and wys."

After a short stay in the Western Highlands, fresh military movements were decided upon by the Scottish leaders. With characteristic boldness they once more took the field, and directed their energies mainly against the English garrisons, which occupied all the formidable castles and strongholds throughout the country. As they advanced fresh reinforcements joined them. While at Dunkeld it was arranged that St Johnston, or Perth, should be attacked. From his intimate knowledge of the locality, Eamsay was consulted by Wallace as to their chances of success in this direction. Eamsay informed him that the walls of the city were low, but the ditch was deep. The latter, however, could be easily filled up, so as to enable a force of a thousand men to be poured into the city at once. At Dunkeld they accordingly remained four days, actively preparing for the coming siege.

By Ramsay's instructions, powerful battering rams were constructed of wood, felled in the forests of Dunkeld, which were to be floated down the river at the appointed time. When all their arrangements were completed they set out for Perth Ramsay acting as guide,. When the Scots had surrounded the city, they proceeded to fill up a portion of the great ditch with earth and stones. After laying over this temporary passage planks of timber on long supporting beams, they succeeded in reaching the walls against which they were enabled to bring their battering rams into play with great effect. Ramsay and Graham stoutly assailed the turret-bridge, while Wallace and his men attacked the mid-side of the city. The Scots were received with great volleys of huge stones and other missiles by the defenders. Notwithstanding the vigorous defence, the Scots swarmed over the walls into the city, and after a severe hand-to-hand conflict the Englishmen were completely defeated. Two thousand of the enemy lay dead in the streets. Sir John Siward, the Governor, fled by river in a light barge with sixty of his chief officers, and sought refuge in the Castle of 1 undee.

After remaining in Perth for three days engaged in despoil- ing the city of its riches and military stores, besides making arrangements for its future defence, Wallace withdrew with the bulk of his forces to carry war throughout the Northern Counties. Marching to Aberdeen, he issued a proclamation summoning the men of that district to join his standard. From this town the Scots, now 4000 strong, proceeded in battle array and with their banners proudly displayed through the Mearns to storm Dunnottar, a stronghold of considerable importance garrisoned by the English. The defenders were at once called upon to surrender the fortress, and informed that their lives would be spared. The terms of surrender were refused, whereupon the Scots, adopting the barbarous methods of warfare initiated by the English at the Barns of Ayr, ruthlessly set fire to the Castle, and a scene of great panic ensued. The defenders had to flee for their lives. Many perished in the flames, others who escaped from the burning castle in despair clung to the rocks, but only to be cut down or thrown headlong into the sea by the infuriated Scots. Not an English soldier survived the flames and the fierce-onslaught of the assailants. After returning to Aberdeen, where they pillaged and burned the English ships, the Scots proceeded to drive out every detachment of the enemy which they discovered throughout the North. The war was thus being prosecuted with marked success. The men of Angus and the Mearns took up arms in great numbers, and were enthusiastic in their support of the national movement. The Castle of Dundee was besieged in the summer of 1297. While encamped on Clatto Moor oatmeal was supplied to the Scottish army from the Mill of Fallaws, at that time within this parish. The spot where this old mill stood is still known by tradition as Wallace's "ruaut barn."

While engaged in the siege of Dundee, intelligence reached the Scottish leaders that a powerful English army, under the Earl of Surrey, was on the inarch to Stirling. Wallace, leaving a detachment of two thousand of the men of Ans; us to continue- the siege, pushed forward the rest of his troops to guard the passage of the Forth. To cope with a force so vastly superior in numbers demanded skilful strategy. Accordingly

Wallace, Graham, and Ramsay devised a plan of battle with the greatest care and ability. It was decided that the Bridge of Stirling then a rude wooden structure spanning the Forth, should be defended at all hazards. Obtaining the services of a country carpenter they ordered him to weaken with his saw the main trestles of the bridge, so that at a given signal the whole structure might easily collapse should any special strain be applied to it. The stratagem was thus carefully and cunningly carried out, and the destruction of the bridge rendered dependent upon the withdrawal of a few wooden bolts. On the day of battle, the English forces were drawn up 50,000 strong the vanguard led by Crcssingham: while the other division was under the command of Warrenne. When Cressingham had led his troops over the bridge in safety and was ready to make the attack, the warning-horn sounded from the Scottish lines, the feeble supports of the bridge in a moment were removed, and with a crash the whole structure was precipitated with its burden of soldiers into the waters of the Forth. The Scots, 10,000 strong, seeing their opportunity, with pike, spear, and sword rushed furiously upon Cressingham's division, and a desperate conflict followed, in which the Scots, under the personal leadership of their Generals, performed prodigies of valour. Cressingham was slain, and his division totally routed. The rest of the enemy fled in consternation from the battlefield, hotly pursued by a detachment of mounted Scots under Ramsay and Boyd, and the retreat was not ended until Warrenne found himself with a fragment of his fugitive forces within the walls of the Castle of Dunbar.

The memorable Battle of Stirling was soon followed by the proclamation of Wallace as Warden of Scotland, and the almost complete evacuation of the country by the invaders. For five months there was a cessation of war throughout Scotland. A Convention of the Estates was summoned to meet at Perth for the consideration of the affairs of the country. This Parliament was attended by most of the chiefs, with the important exception of Cospatrick or Earl Patrick, who, from motives of jealousy, refused to recognise and swear fidelity to the Government established by the national party. Supported by Ramsay, Graham, Boyd, and Lundie, Wallace collected his forces and led them against those who had taken up arms under Earl Patrick, whom they viewed practically as English mercenaries. Several well-contested engagements followed between the rival forces, in all of which Ramsay bore a conspicuous part. This outbreak against the authority of Wallace terminated in the expulsion of Earl Patrick and his supporters from Scotland, and the consolidation of the patriotic party. The triumph of the Scottish leader Avas not yet, however, complete, nor was peace destined long to be maintained. The Scottish nobles who had surrendered to King Edward urgently persuaded him to take immediate action in order to reassert his ascendancy over Scotland. Such counsels inspired a new English invasion. Intelligence of this movement having reached Wallace, he prepared to check it by assembling a great army on Roslin Muir. Selecting 20,000 of his best soldiers, he informed them of the intended invasion, and called upon them to aid him with heart and hand in anticipating the project of the enemy by following him across the border. His chiefs and soldiers enthusiastically responded to his call to do or die.

"The gud Ramsay furth to that jornay went; Schir Jhone the Grayme, forthwart in his entent; Wallace cusyng, Adam, full worthi was, And Robert Boid; full blythly furth thai pass. Baith Awchynlek, and Richard off Lundy, Lawder and Hay, and Cetoun full worthy."

Marching to the South, the Scottish army drew up near Roxburgh Castle, then occupied by the English under Sir Ralph Gray. As there was no time for delay, the Governor was ordered at once to surrender, or run the risk of being hanged over the walls of the fortress. A similar command was despatched with Sir John Ramsay to Berwick. Having crossed the borders, the Scots seized every opportunity of retaliating upon the English for innumerable wrongs.

As they marched through Northumberland desolation followed in their track. The only buildings they spared were churches and abbeys, and of their enemies only women and children. Revenge for former English cruelties and similar atrocities, besides a deeply-rooted spirit of hatred of the Southron, fired every breast. The victorious army, flushed with victory, hurried forward until it reached the massive walls of the city of York. Arranging his army in four divisions, "Wallace-proceeded to invest the city. The southern side was invested by Wallace, the northern by Eamsay; Sir John the Grahame commanded the eastern gate, while Earl Malcolm and Boyd held the western. The siege was conducted and maintained with great vigour. The Scottish infantry, supported by the archers, strained every nerve to get within the walls; but the defenders manned the ramparts in great numbers and offered a most strenuous resistance. Repeatedly the garrison sallied forth to repel the besiegers, but were repulsed with great slaughter. The Scots refused to be beaten off. "With char-acteristic tenacity they struggled for victory.

After a bloody and prolonged struggle a truce was at length concluded, by which the English agreed, without an absolute surrender, to permit the Scottish banner to wave over their walls; to pay down in specie 5000 pounds of English gold; and to furnish what supplies were necessary for the maintenance of the Scottish army. These terms seemed to be quite acceptable to the Scots, as the place was one of great strength, while they were beginning to experience a scarcity of victuals. After remaining at York for twenty days the Scots took their homeward journey, plundering and destroying by fire everything of value that lay in their line of march. Shortly after this encounter a peace was concluded, which was welcome news to a sorely-stricken country. King Edward delivered up the fortresses of York and Berwick to the Scottish army. Ramsay, in return for his distinguished services on the field, was made Governor of Berwick, and Seaton Governor of Roxburgh Castle. On the return of the Scottish army from England the Castle of Dundee was stormed and destroyed, while its Governor, Morton, was hanged.

When war again broke out we find Sir John Ramsay fighting in the Battle of Falkirk (1298), which terminated so disastrously for the Scots. He is mentioned as one of the commanders selected by Wallace to search the battlefield, after the victorious forces withdrew, for the body of the valiant Sir John de Graham. After this reverse Wallace resigned the Guardianship of Scotland.

Throughout the next five years Scotland was very nearly re-conquered by successive invasions. Most of the chiefs had fled, and their forces dispersed. Ramsay and Ruthven alone held out within a fortress at Stockford, in Ross-shire. During the absence of Wallace in France, whither he had gone to enlist French sympathy for Scotland, the alarming intelligence reached him of the English invasion. Accordingly, he set sail for Scotland, and, to the joy of his former chiefs, landed, in the year 1303, at the port of Montrose, with a body of French auxiliaries which he had raised in Flanders. Here he was met by Sir John Ramsay, and other chiefs.

"In Munross hawyn thai brocht hym to the land; Till trew Scottis it was a blithe tithand; Schyr John Ramsay, that worthi was and wycht, Fra Ochtyrhouss the way he chesyt rycht, To meite Wallace with men off amies Strang, Off his duellyng thai had thocht wondyr lang. The trew Ruwan come als with outyn baid, In Barnan wod he had his lugyng maid. Barklay be that to Wallace semblyt fast; With thre hundreth to Ochtyrhouss lie past."

Escorted by Ramsay and his men, Wallace was conducted to Auchterhouse Castle. This interesting episode is also thus recorded:

"Fair wind and weather, nothing worse they fanil, Then at Montrose they safely all do land; Good Sir John Ramsay and the Ruthven true, Barclay and Bisset, with men not a few, Do Wallace meet, all canty, keen, and crouse, And with three hundred march to Ochterhouse."

It is recorded that the Castle of Auchterhouse was occupied on the night of the 20th July 1303 by King Edward during the course of his successful invasion. The English Sovereign, with a great army, had entered Scotland by the western marches. Advancing to Edinburgh, he continued in triumph to Perth, thence to Dundee. From this town he proceeded to Brechin and Aberdeen, and penetrated as far as Morayshire. Having swept the country practically unopposed, and reduced it amid all the horrors of war, besides exacting homage from the northern chiefs, he returned on the 20th of October 1303 to Dundee. It was while on the march to the north that he bestowed his attention upon the Castle of Auchterhouse. From events that subsequently occurred, the bulk of the English forces must have been withdrawn from Dundee by vessels to England.

Shortly after this a considerable body of troops assembled at Birnani Wood under Wallace and Ramsay, which was soon strengthened by detachments of hardy Angus men. With this force the chiefs resolved to attempt the re-capture of Perth, which, like most of the other walled towns of the country, had fallen once more into the enemy's hands. They accordingly marched to Kinnoul, where they halted. It chanced while they lay there that six servants employed by the English garrison had gone from the city to bring home a supply of hay on carts from that locality. While the servants were thus employed the Scots fell upon them, and put them to the sword. The bodies were immediately stripped, and the peasants' dresses assumed by Wallace, Ruthven, Guthrie, Bisset, and other two soldiers. Five soldiers were then placed in each cart, and carefully concealed with hay. Disguised as countrymen, "Wallace and the others proceeded to the city. While this bold stratagem was being carried out, Ramsay with his men was lying in ambush awaiting the signal for the onslaught. The carters having crossed the drawbridges without suspicion, at once threaV off their disguise, the others sprang from their carts all seized their swords, and then with a few strokes the guards were cut down. Thereupon Ramsay and the other Scots rushed in, the garrison was surprised a severe melee ensued, and few of the English escaped with their lives. After the city was thus captured

"Schyr Jhon Ramsay gret captane ordand he, Ruwan Schirreff at ane accord for to be."

Leaving Ramsay and Ruthven in possession of Perth, Wallace, with a small body of troops, set out with his wonted energy to reconnoitre the surrounding country and ascertain the strength of the enemy in Fife. Previous to his departure, however, he left instructions that those officers should join him in the event of any surprise. When this detachment of Scots was on the march, its movements had been watched by Sir John Stewart. Confident of success, Stewart put himself at the head of 1,500 men to cut off this small force. Perceiving the danger and taken by surprise, Wallace withdrew his forces into Black Earnside Forest, where he resolved to hold out till reinforcements came from Perth. Stewart pressed the Scots with great vigour, and was especially eager to effect the capture of Wallace. Fortunately, however, reinforcements from Perth arrived under Eamsay and Ruthven, and soon fortune once more favoured the Scots. Sir John Stewart, who had fought with great bravery, and killed Bisset, a well-known Scottish officer, in a hand-to-hand encounter, was slain by Wallace, and his forces routed. Subsequently, Eamsay also re-captured the Castle of Cupar, and took part in other engagements. Notwithstanding the defections and jealousies of many of the nobles, he remained loyal to Wallace until the latter was basely betrayed, and afterwards executed on the 23rd August 1305. After the death of Wallace history is silent regarding the latter deeds of Sir John Ramsay. His name does not appear amongst those who suffered death at the time of Wallace's capture, nor is it mentioned among the slain in subsequent conflicts. Whether he died sword in hand in the future wars, or within his own castle, is unknown. From the fact that the aisle within the-church was long known as the Eamsay aisle, it is not unlikely that he died at Auchterhouse Castle, and was buried within the old church. Unquestionably, Sir John was an able and valiant knight, and a man who served his country most faithfully in times of great national danger and perplexity. He was ever the foe of the English oppressors, the true friend of freedom's cause, and his fame as a Scottish chief ought only to be forgotten when the memory of the great struggle for national independence is itself obliterated.

The fragmentary ruins of the old castle of Auchterhouse, the stronghold of the Eamsay family, may still be seen, thickly overgrown with ivy, standing on a rock beside a stream. The ruins are well known as the Wallace Tower, in honour of the great patriot's visit. From the present aspect of the ruins, the walls of which are about 12 feet in thickness, the original building, which covered a considerable extent of ground, must have been of great strength. The roof of the ground floor had been strongly arched, and in one side there is an arched door, about 5 feet high and 4 feet wide. There is also a very food example of a window or light-hole after the Scoto-ISTorman style of architecture. The castle appears to have been constructed after the massive style of architecture adopted by the ScokkNorman Barons. When Ave look upon this grey relic of former feudal times, and recall its noble occupant, and the name of his still more illustrious compatriot, we are reminded of of these lines

"In many a Castle, town, and plain, Mountain and forest still remain; Fondly cherished spots which claim The proud distinction of his honoured name, Swells the huge ruin's massy heap, In castled court, 'tis Wallace's keep."

About the year 1300, Sir William de Euthven, another of the Scottish chiefs, was married to Marjory, daughter of Sir John Ramsay. In 1309, King Robert Bruce granted a charter to Sir William Ramsay of 416 acres of the land of Ingilstone. He fought at Bannockburn, and was one of the Scottish Barons who attended the Parliament convened by the King at Arbroath in 1320, to frame an answer to the threatened excommunication by the Pope. His signature is attached to the famous historical document which asserted the national independence, and declared that " so long as there shall but one hundred of us remain alive, we will never submit ourselves to the dominion of England. For it is not glory, they also declared; it is not riches, neither is it honour; but it is liberty alone that we fight and contend for, which no honest man will lose but with his life."

Sir John Ramsay left a son, named Alexander, who was recognised as the " flower of courtliness." He occupied a distinguished position as a soldier in the time of the Bruce. In war he was reckoned one of the bravest of men, and in times of peace was accounted one of the most courteous men of his day. Bannockburn having been fought and won, and Scotland free, the exultant Scottish soldiers, under the command of the chivalrous and impetuous Edward Bruce, threw themselves into the struggle of liberating Ireland also from the yoke of the English invader. Among the knights who won for themselves high renown in the achieve- ments of that eventful and romantic war was Sir Alexander Ramsay of Ochterhous.

' He Edward Bruce had thar in hys sumpany The Erie Thomas that wes worthy; And gud Schyr Philip the Mowbray, That sekyr wes in hard affay: Schyr Jhone the Souths ane gud Knycht; And Schyr Jhone Stewart that wes wycht. The Ramsay als off Ouchtrehouss, That wes wycht and cheivalrouss; And Schyr Eergus off Adrossane: And othyr Knychts mony ane."

Sir Alexander commanded a division at the Battle of Carrick-fergus in 1315, when the enemy was repulsed with great slaughter. He was also present at the storming and sacking of Dundalk, and served until the termination of the Avar. After the death of the great Bruce, the name of Sir Alexander Eamsay is frequently mentioned in connection with the fierce struggles which ensued with the English throughout the Regency. In 1335, while associated in command with the Earl of Moray, he surprised and defeated, on the Borough Muir, near Edinburgh, a body of French troops which had come to the assistance of the English. The Castle of Edinburgh thereafter capitulated, notwithstanding the resolute bravery of the defenders, who had piled up the carcases of their horses and employed them as ramparts.

In 1337-8 the. Castle of Dunbar, then one of the strongest in the country, was closely besieged by sea and land by the English forces, under the Earl of Salisbury. Its defence Avas conducted with great ability, courage, and perseverance, in the absence of the Earl of March, by his high-spirited Countess, better known in history as "Black Agnes." For five months this plucky and eccentric heroine resisted all the efforts of the besiegers so determinedly that at length the English resolved to starve the garrison into surrender. This, however, was frustrated by the timeous arrival of Kamsay, who, with a body of resolute Scots, broke through the enemy's lines during the darkness of the night, and reached the Castle with a welcome supply of provisions for its defenders, who, from the persistency and completeness of the siege, had suffered great privations.

Kamsay and his troops afterwards attacked the advanced guards of the enemy, and drove them back. The English were at length compelled to abandon the siege and withdraw their forces, deeply chagrined at the unsuccessful issue of the blockade.

After the English leader's departure for the South, the Avar was prosecuted with great success by the Scottish leaders, Douglas and Kamsay. "While the Douglas the fiery Knight of Liddesdale was driving the English before him in Teviotdale, Kamsay had taken up a strong position among the crags and caves of Hawthornden, on the banks of the Esk, at the head of a strong body of patriotic Scots drawn from all ranks of society. Under Ramsay, high and low, rich and poor, fought shoulder to shoulder in defence of the Fatherland against the English. From their rocky fastnesses they sallied forth on many occasions, routed the enemy, and compelled them, through dread of this guerilla mode of warfare, to maintain themselves within their castles. Encouraged by his numerous successes, Ramsay at length carried the Avar over the border, and laid Avaste the English territory Avith fire and SAVord. Fordun says " that to be of Alexander Ramsay's band Avas considered a branch of military education requisite for all young gentlemen aviio meant to excel in arms." On one occasion while returning heavily laden Avith booty from Northumberland, the Scots Avere encountered by a strong body of English. Feigning flight, Ramsay succeeded in decoying the English into an ambuscade, Avhere they were attacked and routed, Avhile their commander, Lord Manners, Avas taken prisoner. Encounters of this character Avere, according to the custom of the time, frequently varied by personal combats in presence of the rival forces. A challenge Avas on one occasion issued to the renoavned Knight of Liddesdale by the English

Commander, Henry of Lancaster, and at once accepted by him. In the combat the Douglas was so severely wounded that he was compelled to desist. Another challenge was afterwards sent to Sir Alexander Ramsay by Henry to meet him at a tilting match at Berwick, the conditions being twenty knights a-sicle. They accordingly met, and a stubborn and sanguinary conflict ensued between the chosen representatives of northern and southern chivalry. Two of the English knights were slain, and a Scottish Baron Sir John de Hay-was also killed. Sir William Ramsay, a relative of Sir Alexander, was so severely run through the helmet with a spear that the helmet was completely rivetted to his head by the spear point. Sir Alexander requested him to lie down, and placing his foot on the helmet he drew out the broken spear. Such were the days of chivalry, and such were the thrilling personal encounters in which the barons bold delighted. Through the military prowess of Douglas and Ramsay, the English armies were soon completely driven from the open country, and compelled to confine themselves to their fortresses. On the 30th March 1342 Sir Alexander gallantly captured the Castle of Roxburgh by a daring midnight escalade, and as a reward for his distinguished military services King David II. created him Governor of Roxburgh Castle, and assigned to him the rich lands of Teviotdale. This appointment, however, proved to be an impolitic one, because it roused the fury and jealousy of the Douglas, who considered that the lands assigned by the King to Ramsay were under his special jurisdiction. Henceforth he became the implacable enemy of Ramsay, and eagerly sought revenge. In the discharge of his duties as High Sheriff, Sir Alexander had occasion to summon the Crown vassals to a meeting in the Church of Hawick. To this meeting Douglas, with a strong body of armed retainers went, and was courteously received by Ramsay. While the business was being conducted, Ramsay, however, was surprised, treacherously attacked and wounded by Douslas, while at the same time three of his men were cut c down. Thrown bleeding across his horse, he was escorted over a wild and dreary district to Hermitage Castle, one of the strongholds of Douglas, lying amid the morasses of Liddesdale, and there thrown into a dungeon and left to starve to death. Here he supported existence for seventeen days by means of particles of corn which fell through the crevices of a granary floor above his prison; but at length he succumbed to starvation. This was an atrocious crime, and a terrible death for one who was recognised as one of the ablest soldiers in the early Scottish wars. Four hundred and fifty years afterwards, a mason, in excavating round the front of Hermitage Castle, laid open a stone vault, about eight feet square, in which, amid a heap of chaff and dust, lay several human bones, along with a large and powerful bridle-bit and an ancient sword. These were understood to have been the mournful relics of this barbarous incident of a so-called chivalrous age. Thus perished in 1342 a knight whom the historian of the times designates " one of the bravest, and worthiest, and most fortunate leaders of the Scottish nation, to the everlasting infamy of him who perpetrated the murder." He had done a great deal, says Fordun, for the King and for the country's freedom; he had felled the foe everywhere around, greatly checked their attacks, won many a victory, done much good, and, so far as man can judge, would have done more had he lived longer. In brave deeds of arms and in bodily strength he surpassed all others of his day.

Wynton passes the following eulogium upon him: " He was the greatest menyd man That any could have thought on than; Of his state or of more by far, All menyt (lamented) him, baith better and waur, The rich and puir him menyde baith, For of his dede (death) was meikle skaith."

It is a melancholy reflection, says Tytler, that a fate so horrid befel one of the bravest and most popular leaders of the Scottish nation, and that the deed did not only pass unrevenged, but that the perpetrator received a speedy pardon, and was rewarded to the very office which led to the murder. According to the custom of the age of chivalry, all those who followed the banner of a great baron who fell by treachery were bound to seek satisfaction with the sword from all in any way associated with the deed. The terrible fate of Ramsay, accordingly, led to innumerable feuds, dissensions, and sanguinary struggles among the great families of Scotland. In revenge for this base treachery and foul murder, the Knight of Liddesdale was subsequently waylaid and assassinated by his cousin and god-son William, afterwards Earl of Douglas, while hunting in the forest of Ettrick in 1353. With all his faults, Fordun says he was a hardy soldier, and one who had endured much in the defence of the liberty of the kingdom skilled in war, faithful to his promise, the scourge of the English, and a wall of defence to Scotland. The memory of Sir Alexander Ramsay is thus embalmed by Henry

"His sone Sir John's was cald the flour of courtlyness, As witness weill in to the schort tretty Eftir the Bruce, quha redis in that story. He rewlit weill bathe in to wer and pes: Alexander Ramsay, to nayme he hecht, but les. Quhen it wes wer, till amies he hirn kest; Wndir the croun he was ane off the best; In time of pees till courtlyness he zeid: Bot to gentrice he tuk nayne othir heid. Quhat gentill man had nocht with

Ramsay beyne; Off courtlynes thai cownt him nocht a preyne. Fiedome and treuth lie had as men would ass; Sen he begane na bettyr squier was. Roxburgh hauld he wan full manfully; Syne held it lang, quhill tratouris tresonably Causit his dede, I can nocht tell you how, Off sic thingis I will ga by as now."

This lamented hero and patriot left a son well-known as Sir William Ramsay. From what is recorded of him he seems to have inherited much of his father's military capacity and passion for arms. His name was a familiar one among the knights of the reign of King David II. On one occasion he was despatched by the Earl of March on an armed expedition into England, and over-ran Northumberland. He destroyed Norham, and when in the act of parading his spoils before the eyes of the defenders of Norham Castle, he was perceived by Sir Thomas Gray of Chillingham, Governor of Norbam, who sallied out from the Castle to terminate the depredations of the Scots. Retiring, hotly pursued across the Tweed by the English horsemen, Ramsay skilfully succeeded in drawing the pursuers into a carefully-prepared ambuscade held by the Earl of March. The English, finding themselves entrapped and surrounded, fought with great valour, but were finally beaten. The Governor was taken prisoner, and his force annihilated. As a bold and successful raider, Sir William ranked high among the hardy soldiers of his time. A descendant, Sir Alexander Ramsay, was killed at the battle of Homildon in 1402. His son, also named Sir Alexander, was one of the distinguished Scottish barons commissioned to proceed to England in 1423 to form an escort to James I. on his return to Scotland after his long captivity in England. In return for his services to his sovereign he was knighted at his coronation on the following year. For many years the representatives of this old and distinguished Scottish family continued to hold the Sheriffships of Angus, and to maintain their reputation for chivalry and pure and disinterested patriotism. Robert Ramsay of Auchterhouse was Sheriff of Angus, 9th April 1359. John was collector of one of the quarters of Angus in 1359. King David II. granted a charter to Malcolm Ramsay of the lands of Mains. Subsequently the Sheriffships of Angus was held by Sir Walter Ogilvie of Powrie, who had married in 1380 Isabella, the only child of Sir Malcolm Ramsay, and thus became proprietor of the lands of Auchterhouse. Like many of the chiefs of his time, Sir Walter fell in battle. Duncan Stewart, better known as the "Wolf of Badenoch," natural son of Alexander, Earl of Buchan, Laving entered the shire of Angus at the head of a lawless hand of robbers, with the intention of pillaging the country, the High Sheriff, accompanied by his natural brother, Walter Leighton, overtook them at a place called Glencune or Glenbeith, near Blairgowrie, and after a sharp skirmish, Sir Walter Ogilvie, Leighton, and about sixty of their followers were slain. Sir Walter is often designated

"Sir Walter Ogilvy, that brave knicht, Stout and manful, bauld and wicht."

From him were descended the families of Auchterhouse, Lin-trathen, and Inverquharity. His son, Sir Walter, was also slain at the battle of Harlaw on the 24th July 1411. This battle was fought during the regency of the Duke of Albany between Donald, Lord of the Isles, and the Earl of Mar. At the head of an army of ten thousand Celtic warriors, Donald had carried Avar throughout the northern Highlands, and was preparing also to pillage and lay waste the district south of the Grampians. At Harlaw, near Aberdeen, he was encountered by a force under the Earl of Mar, which comprised the elite of the Angus barons and knights, with a strong muster of their retainers. It appears to have been an obstinate and bloody contest, from the description given of it in the old ballad of the " Battle of Harlaw" (traditionary version):

"On Munonday at morning
The battle it began,
On Saturday at gloamin'
Ye'd scarce tell wha had wan.
And sic a weary burying
The like ye never saw, As there was the Sunday after that
On the Muirs down by Harlaw.
And if Hielan' lasses speer at ye
For them that gaed awa, Ye may tell them plain and plain enough
They're sleeping at Harlaw."

The battle terminated in the defeat of the Highlanders of the north-west, and secured the undoubted supremacy of the Lowlanders. Victory was dearly purchased, however, as many of the principal barons of Angus fell.

"Of the best among them was
The gracious gucle Lord Ogilvy, The Sheriff-Principal of Angus,
Renowned for truth and equitie, For faith and magnanimitie;
He had few fallows in the field, Yet fell by fatal destiny,
For he naeways wou'd grant to yield."

Amongst those who were knighted by King James I. on the day of his coronation at Perth was Patrick Ogilvie of Auchter-house, brother of the late Sir Walter. The oath taken on such great occasions has been preserved, and is of much historical interest:

1. I shall fortify and defend the Christian religion to the uttermost of my power.

2. I shall be loyal and true to my Sovereign Lord the King; to all orders of chivalry, and to the noble office of arms.

3. I shall fortify and defend justice at my power, and that without favour or enmity.

4. I shall never flee from my Sovereign Lord the King, nor from his lieutenants, in time of affray or battle.

5. I shall defend my native realm from all aliens and strangers.

6. I shall defend the just action and quarrel of all ladies of honour, of all true and friendless widows, of orphans, and of maidens of good fame.

7. I shall do diligence wheresoever I hear that there are any murderers, traitors, or masterful robbers, who oppress the King's lieges or poor people, to bring them to the law at my power.

8. I shall maintain and uphold the noble state of chivalry with horse, armour, and other knightly habiliments, and shall help and succour those of the same order at my power if they have need.

9. I shall enquire and seek to have the knowledge and understanding of all the art and points contained in the books of chivalry.

All these pi'omises to observe, keep, and fulfil I oblige me, so help me God, by my own hand, and by Cod himself.

These were days of constant warfare. Every man was a soldier, and bound to follow the banner of his lord. Every other occupation but that of arms was despised. Awe and obedience to the Sovereign and barons were exacted at the point of the sword. In the early Scottish wars the favourite weapon was the pike. The chiefs wore plate armour, and carried the two-handed sword, battleaxe, and mace. King James I., with the view of encouraging dexterity in the use of the bow and arrow, ordered shooting butts to be erected near the Parish Churches, where competitions might be regularly engaged in. He was most anxious to introduce this weapon among the Lowland Scots, as the prowess of the English archers had been established on many battlefields. The Scots, however, preferred to adhere to the favourite national weapon, the pike. To promote the practice in archery, the King further prohibited the games of golf and football. By the Parliament of 1458 (King James II.), it is decreed and ordained that the displays of weapons be held by the lords and barons, spiritual and temporal, four times in the year; that the football and golf be utterly cried down and not be used; that the bow-marks be made, a pair of butts at every Parish Church, and shooting-be practised; that every man shoot six shots at the least, and that twopence be levied upon the absent for drink to the shooters. If the parish be large, there shall be three, four, or five bow-marks in the most convenient places, and that all men exceeding twelve and under fifty years of age practice archery.

The old archery ground of this parish, still well-known by the name of the " Bow Butts,"' may still be seen on the lands of Templeton. Such sports developed the warlike spirit of a restless people, whose chief enjoyment in life seemed centred in arms. We can easily understand how the annals of the period are entirely occupied with the tales of bloodshed, the settling of private feuds, the hatching of conspiracies and quarrels, or the still more popular one of plundering and foraging across the border.

Sir Patrick Ogilvie was one of the nobles arrested for conspiracy by order of King James I., along with the Duke of Albany. He was, however, soon released, and restored to the royal favour. As Sheriff of Angus and Great Justiciary of Scotland, he was a member of an important Embassy to the Court of France. In May 1425 he served as one of the jury of the nobility which condemned to death the Duke of Albany, his two sons, and the Earl of Lennox. After the death of Stewart of Darnley in 1429, he was also appointed Constable of the Scottish army in France. On the 14th April 1426 James I. confirmed grant by Patrick de Ogilvie, Knt., with consent of his father, Alexander de Ogilvie, Sheriff of Forfar, of certain rents from lands in Banffshire, to found a Chaplainry in the Chapel of the Blessed Virgin M ry of Garvoch: if the rents are not forthcoming from this property they are to be uplifted from the baronial lands of Auchterhouse and Eassie. Feb. 26, 1439, King James II. confirmed charters dated at Auchterhouse 10th March 1438, whereby Margaret de Fenton of Beaufort grants certain lands to Walter Ogilby, son of the late Sir Patrick de Ogilby of Auchterhouse. March 28, 1453, King James II. confirmed letters given by Alex, de Ogilvy of Auchterhouse, Sheriff of Forfar, to his brother, Walter of Ogilvy of Beaufort, appointing him manager of all his estates. The original letters are in Scottish, and were written at Auchterhouse.

Be it kend till al men be thir present lettrez, me, Alexander of Ogilvy of Uchterhouse, Shiref of Forfar ande of Banf, tie have gevin and grantit, c, to my derrast brother, Walter of Ogilvy of Beuforte, the hale governance in al thyngs of myne anne person to be in his speciale keping, conservasione, ande yeme for al the dais of my lyve or his lyve, with full power and governance of al and sindri my landis, possessiones, and annuell rentis, with the pertinantis had and for to be had within the realme of Scotland qnhaeresumever; and al tha said landis to set, and the malis of them to rais and ressave at his anne lyking; with full power of bailyery of thaim for al the dais of his lyve; all strengthis, housis, castellis, or toweris pertenande or langande to me, or yit be ony manere off' way in tyme to cum be richt of my heritage may happen or fall to me, or richt wisly may pertene to be fully and haly in the saide Walter of Ogilvy, my derrast brother's keeping, yemesale, and governance, enduring al the dais of the saide Walter's lyve; and al and sundry my gudis, moveblez and unmoveblez, had and for to be had quhaeresumever, and to be frely ressavit, uptakyn, governit, and fullely disponit at the will, desposicion, ande ordinance of the saide Walter, without obstakill, impediment, questionne, or demande of ony man or woman of lyne, enduring the saide date. All and sindri my offices of Sherifdomes of Forfar and Banf, with all and sindri profittis or avalis to the saide officis pertenande or may pertene, to be usit, occupyit, ande fullely governyt be the saide Walter of Ogilvy, or his deputis, substitutis, under him for al the dais of his lyve, all my tenantis, indwellaris, or yit inhabitantis, of all and sindri my landis had or for to be had at the verray maintenance and governance of the said Walter enduring the said date; and hereaftour I, the saide Alexander of Ogilvy, bindis ande lebly and treuly oblisis me be the faithe and laute in my body, withoute fraude or gile, to stand, bide, and stedfastly to remayne at the very ful governance of my said brother in al and sindri powntis and articlis as is before writin for al the dais of my lyve, na I sal never revoke nor yet againcal na kynde of condicion na appoyntment above writtin, but sal lebly and treuly keep thaim and ger them be kepit the saide condicions and appoyntments to the utterest, withoute fraude or gile. In the witnessing of the quhilk thing my sele is hungyn to this my present writt.

At Uchterhous.

March, 17, 1452.

On the 23rd January, 1446, there occurred one of those sanguinary struggles for supremacy characteristic of the age between the Ogilvies and Lindsays. This is known historically as the battle of Arbroath. The Earl of Crawford, a powerful and ambitious baron, well known for his restless, predatory character, had seized and appropriated certain lands belonging to Kennedy, the Bishop of St Andrews, and subsequently formed the intention of enriching himself at the expense of the Abbey of Arbroath. This audacious and sacrilegious project aroused the hostility of the Ogilvies, who were determined to adopt strong measures to curb the avarice of Crawford. Mustering to their full clan strength, admirably mounted, and fully equipped for war, they proceeded to Arbroath to defend with their lives the rights and possessions of the ancient sacred establishment. While the Ogilvies had constituted themselves guardians of the Abbey, the Earl of Huntly, with his military retinue, chanced to arrive there on his return from the Court, and, according to the custom of the age, was hospitably received and entertained by the Chapter. Having learned from the Ogilvies of the Earl of Crawford's anticipated attack, Huntly, as a valiant son of the Church, joined them, and they rode forth together to encounter the redoubtable Lindsay, who was in the neighbourhood at the head of his retainers. As the rival forces were strongly represented, a fiercely-contested battle followed. When the day was over, five hundred horsemen lay stretched upon the field, including many representatives of Angus chivalry. The Earl of Crawford was among the slain, while on the other side Huntly met the same fate. The Laird of Airlie, the chief of the Ogilvies, was taken prisoner by the Master of Crawford, better known subsequently as the notorious Earl " Beardie." Although the victory, so far, went in favour of the Ogilvies, it was followed by terrible reprisals on the part of the Lindsays, who, supported by the Douglases, overran their lands, burnt their castles, and hunted them down with relentless barbarity.

Sir Alexander Ogilvy of Auchterhouse, son of Sir Walter, had an only daughter, Margaret, who was married to James Stewart, surnamed " Hearty James," the grandson of Sir James Stewart, the " Black Knight of Lome," by Jane Beaufort, Queen of Scotland, the widow of King James I., and the mother of King James II. James Stewart succeeded upon the fall of Lord Boyd to the office of High Chamberlain of Scotland in 1471. In 1473, he resigned this appointment on being sent as Ambassador to the Court of France. On his return to Scotland he was made Warden of the East Marches, and afterwards re-appointed to the post of Lord High Chamberlain.

When the English army, under the Duke of Gloucester, invaded Scotland in 1482, to place the Duke of Albany on the Scottish throne, King James III. mustered his forces and proceeded with all haste towards the Borders to intercept the further advance of the enemy. While encamped at Lauder, several of the chief nobles of Scotland, amongst whom was James, Earl of Buchan, boldly entered the King's tent, and informed him of their dissatisfaction with his conduct in acting so inimically to the highest interests of his country, by refusing countenance to the leading nobles, and in making favourites of certain individuals of low birth and worthless character, upon whom he had bestowed titles, and also raised to the rank of Privy Counsellors. These strong remonstrances were followed up immediately by actions of a sterner character, for the turbulent nobles seized the royal favourites and hanged them over the Bridge of Lauder. Thereafter, the King was escorted to Edinburgh Castle, placed under guard, and a peace concluded between the English Commander and the high-spirited nobles. Subsequently, the Earl of Buchan sided with the Duke of Albany, and was prominently connected with many of the conspiracies, revolts, and turmoils which characterized that unhappy reign. In 1466, the Earldom of Buchan, one of the oldest of the Scottish titles, and one previously held by members of the Eoyal Family, was conferred upon him. By his marriage with Margaret Ogilvy, he became proprietor of the lands of Auchterhouse. In 1469 he took the title of Lord Auchterhouse, which is still held by the present representative of the Earldom.

Sept. 22, 1478. James III. grants to his uncle, by his mother's side avunculus), James, Earl of Buchan and Lord of Auchterhouse, the lands of Auchterhouse, with Castle, c.; Nevay, Eassie, Kynnalty, and Kettins, c, c, which had

"been resigned by the said Earl and his Countess, Margaret de Ogilvy.

Feb. 18, 1482-3. James III. confirms a charter, dated at Auchterhouse 21st August 1478, by Sir Alexander Ogilvy, Sheriff of Forfar, granting the lands of Balkerry in Eassie to William de Fenton and his wife, Matilda Kamsay, sister of Sir Alexander.

June 27, 1489. James IV. grants to his avunculus, James, Earl of Buchan and Lord of Auchterhouse, certain lands in Forfar, which had been forfeited by Robert, Lord Lyle, and which were united to the Barony of Auchterhouse.

May 20, 1491. James IV. confirms a charter by James, Earl of Buchan, of certain lands in the Barony of Auchterhouse to Alexander Stewart and Isabel Ogilvy, his wife.

May 19, 1492. James IV. confirms a charter by James, Earl of Buchan, conferring the Barony of Auchterhouse, with the Castle, on his first-born son, Alexander Stewart. One of the witnesses is David, Abbot of Arbroath. The date on charter is 21st Jan. 1490.

Feb. 6, 1499. James IV. confirms certain lands in the Barony of Auchterhouse to Alexander, Earl of Buchan, and Margaret Euthven, his wife. James, Earl of Buchan, died in 1500, leaving a son who became his successor. Of the second and third Earls of Buchan there is little known of any historical interest.

April 29, 1525. James V. confirms a charter by John, Earl of Buchan, dated at Auchterhouse, 28th April 1525.

June 15, 1526. James V. confirms charter by John, Earl of Buchan, to his cousin, James Bruce of Rait, of the lands of Bonnytoun of Auchterhouse, dated at Auchterhouse 10th June 1526.

May 30, 1528. James V. confirms charter by John, Earl of Buchan, of lands in Aberdeenshire to James Gordon of Mildmar, dated at Auchterhouse 15th Sept. 1527.

August 12, 1528 James V. confirms the Barony and Lord-ship of Auchterhouse and certain lands in Banff and Aberdeen, to John, Earl of Buchan, uniting them into the free Barony of Glendorroquhy, with the Castle of Banff as principal messuage.

Feb. 18, 1534-5. James Y. confirms a charter by John, Earl of Buchan, dated at Auchterhouse 10th Nov. 1534.

Oct. 30, 1538. James V. decrees that Boneyton of Auchterhouse shall be given to John, Earl of Crawford, as security for a debt owing by John, Earl of Buchan.

March 26, 1543. Queen Mary confirms charter by the late David, Earl of Crawford, of the lands of Boneyton to John Lundy, son of Walter Lundy of that Ilk.

May 15, 1547. Queen Mary confirms a charter by John, Earl of Buchan, to his son, Alexander Stewart, and his wife, Margaret Ogilvy, of certain lands in Banff, dated at Auchterhouse, 29th April 1547.

August 4, 1547. Queen Mary grants Novodamus of Auchterhouse, c, to John Stewart, son and heir apparent of John, Earl of Buchan.

John, 4th Earl of Buchan, fell at the disastrous battle of Pinkie, fought in Sept. 1517, in which the flower of the Scottish nobility perished.

June 4, 1549. Queen Mary grants certain lands in Auchterhouse to James Stewart, son of John, Earl of Buchan.

John, Fourth Earl of Buchan, was twice married first, to Lady Mary Stewart, only child of James, Earl of Moray; secondly, to Margaret, daughter of Walter Ogilvie of Powrie. By the latter he had one child, Christian. Her parents having died, the young heiress of the House of Buchan was placed, while she was a child of only three years of age, under the guardianship of the well-known and historically notorious family of the House of Douglas, who occupied Loch Leven Castle. The lady under whose immediate protection she was placed was Lady Douglas, paramour of King James V., and the mother of the Eegent Moray. This lady has obtained an unenviable place in history from the fact that she was the bitter enemy of Mary, Queen of

Scots. She was not only a woman of dissolute character, but a cool, ambitious, and daring intriguer. While the young, ill-starred child Christian was under her care, a matrimonial contract was skilfully concocted between her and the Regent Moray through the sharp practice of Lady Douglas. This enabled Moray to obtain possession of the valuable estates of Christian. This seems to have been very inconsistent conduct on the part of one who was recognised as a valiant upholder of the Protestant faith, and lauded as one of the greatest of the reforming nobles. With his other excellencies of character, Moray seems to have been the possessor of a hard and avaricious temperament. Notwithstanding this contract and consequent seizure of the revenues of the Buchan estates, the Regent did not hesitate to enter into a matrimonial alliance with a lady of the House of Keith. For years the young and unhappy Christian, isolated from the outer world, remained practically a prisoner within the walls of Loch Leven Castle, while Moray lived in the enjoyment of her revenues. After the marriage of the Regent Moray, Lady Douglas succeeded in effecting a marriage between Christian and her second son, Sir Robert Douglas. This union, however, did not prevent the good Regent from retaining most of the Buchan lands. After her marriage with Sir Robert Douglas, the young Countess still continued to reside at Loch Leven. The castle was frequently visited at this time by Queen Mary in the course of periodical State journeys through her dominions. Shortly after her marriage with Darnley, the Queen proceeded thither with a strong military escort to demand the surrender of the castle, as the family was believed to be one of those in active rebellion against her. The intelligence, however, having been conveyed to her that the Countess of Buchan was at the time in a very delicate state of health, she very generously refrained from taking such extreme measures against the conspirators as she otherwise would have done. Not many months after this visit the Queen Avas accompanied thither as prisoner by Lindsay and Ruthven, and committed to the custody of her inveterate enemies. During the residence of the Countess of Buchan, therefore, in Loch Leven Castle, Queen Mary was also undergoing her memorable period of harsh imprisonment within the same walls, and there appears to have existed the most affectionate intercourse, doubtless strengthened by misfortune, between the unfortunate Queen and the sadly victimised and despoiled Countess. It is believed that, through the instrumentality of Christian, Queen Mary Avas enabled to acquaint her friends at the Court of France of the vicissitudes and wrongs which had befallen her.

13 Feb. 1573-4. James VI. granted Auchterhouse, c, to Robert Stewart, apparent of Todlaw, having been resigned by Christian, Countess of Buchan, with consent of Robert Douglas, Earl of Buchan.

Christian, Countess of Buchan, died in 1580. Her husband, Sir Robert Douglas, who took the title of Earl of Buchan, Avas pronounced in his hostility to Queen Mary. After the assassination of the Regent Moray, and the execution of Archbishop Hamilton for participation in the murder of Damley, the Earl was one of the Scottish nobles who took an active part in the intrigues, factions, and troubles which rendered the reign of Queen Mary so prolific of misfortune to her and her kingdom. He Avas present Avhen the Queen landed at Loch Leven Castle. as prisoner, and was one of those to Avhom she was consigned. His name appears in several of the proclamations issued by Morton, of whose policy he was a zealous supporter. He was one of the eleven nobles taken prisoner by the Loyalists at Stirling in 1575, and by them escorted with his confederates to Edinburgh. With the exception of Morton, aviio Avas fatally wounded, the other nobles were subsequently rescued by a party of musketeers, under the Earl of Mar, when they reached the city. In the following year he was despatched by the Regent in command of a strong body of troops against the Loyalists, who had assembled at Brechin, under Sir Adam Gordon of Auchindown, brother of the Marquis of Huntly. The Earl was, however, defeated, and compelled to retreat, having lost about 50 of his men, while 150 were taken prisoners. He died in 1583. His brother, Sir William Douglas, was implicated in the murder of Kizzio, and his other brother, Sir George, has found a place in history as the deliverer of Queen Mary from her cruel imprisonment within Loch Leven Castle. The Earl left a son, who became Fifth Earl of Buchan. He appears to have been a young nobleman of much promise, of considerable personal attractions, and of exceptional accomplishments. He died, greatly lamented, at the early age of 21, and was buried within Auchterhouse Church. Sir James Balfour wrote the following epitaph upon him:

Hie jacet ante diem lachrimoso funere raptus, Flos patriae et gentis splendor Duglassidornm.

Here lies, prematurely snatched away by a mournful death, The flower of his country and the splendour of the family of the Douglasses.

In the first account of Dundee, which appeared in the reign of King James VI., 1597, Auchterhouse is mentioned as the principal residence of the Earl of Buchan. James, Fifth Earl of Buchan, left one daughter, Marie Douglas, who succeeded to the title. She is said to have been amiable, accomplished, and beautiful, and from her portraits, which still exist, there can be no doubt about the charms of her personal appearance. She was married to James Erskine, eldest son by second marriage of John, Earl of Mar, who, according to the practice of the period, assumed the title of Earl of Buchan. The family of Mar had formerly been connected with the parish, as they were the proprietors of the lands of Dronlaw. It is a family which has figured very conspicuously in their country's history. It was closely allied to the Koyal Family, and for five generations appear to have possessed the custody of the heir to the throne during his nonage. Alexander, second Lord Erskine, was intrusted with the keeping of James IV. in his youth. John,

Fourth Lord, had charge of the young King James Y. John, Fifth Lord, had the infant Prince James at his birth committed to his care by Queen Mary, where he remained, notwithstanding the opposition of Bothwell.

In the year 1G21, when the Five Articles of Perth came to be ratified by Parliament, three of the Scottish nobles the Farls of Buchan, Morton, and Viscount Hamilton refrained from voting. The Earl of Buchan, it is said, was only prevented from voting against the obnoxious acts by the stern interference of his father, the Earl of Mar. It is related how this high-spirited young nobleman, the founder of a family remarkable for its zeal in behalf of civil liberty, expressed his vexation at this paternal interference by bursting into a flood of tears. Straloch in his papers states, however, that this was denied afterwards by the Earl, and from what we know of his subsequent career, no doubt Straloch was correct, as the high-spirited young noble soon developed into a full-blown typical Cavalier, and a devoted supporter of the Royalist policy. He was in high favour with King James VI., and in the Court of King Charles I. held the position of Gentleman of the Bedchamber. He was a prominent figure in the more remarkable state pageants of the period. On the memorable day of the Coronation of King Charles I. as Sovereign of Scotland (18th June 1633), the Earl, as sword-bearer, accompanied by the Earl of Rothes, as sceptre-bearer, headed the Royal procession from the Castle of Edinburgh to the Chapel of Holyrood, where the Coronation ceremony was performed with befitting splendour. From his character, he appears to have been a man whose special qualifications would be serviceable in a Court where craft, insincerity, and duplicity ranked as virtues. He appears to have been one of the confidential agents of the King, and engaged in some of that statecraft and wily diplomacy which subsequently cost his Sovereign his head. It is commonly believed that he accompanied the Duke of Buckingham and Prince Charles on a special matrimonial mission to the Court of D

Spain. In a curious letter, which is of some historical value, it is not difficult to detect the peculiarities and foibles of the gay Cavalier, and the delicate character of some of the negotiations conducted by him for his Koyal Master:

"From James, Earl of Buchan, to his Mother, the Countess of Mar.

Paris, 4th June 1638.

Madam, My departure from England was so sudden that I had scarce time to write that short letter I wrote to your ladyship. Then, now, madam, be pleased to know that I have been here those three months about some of my master's affairs, and by his command I am going within this fortnight to Spain. It is not pertinent for me to write more particularly; but if I had the honour and happiness to be with you I would let you know what whereat I know you would be glad of. Thei'e befel me here ane most unfortunate accident, for being in sleep in my bed about midnight I was almost burnt in my bed before I was aware. Yet I thanked God I escaped, only being a little scalded; but my misfortune was that the greatest part of my moneys I had for my provision I lost before T could g3t time to save any. I think the fire was so violent nobody could venture to save anything. This has put me to my shifts, so that I am forced to borrow moneys for my provision, and could have none but from Scots merchants, so that it must be paid in Scotland. If your ladyship knew the pain I am in you would pity me, for Saturday I have received letters from the King to be gone, so that of necessity I must obey, and I have no other remedy to be extorcioned by our Scots merchants here. Now, madam, believe this as I am a Christian, it stands me no less than my mine, my honour, and reputation, the repayment of those moneys; how much there shall be of it you shall know in my next; and, madam, for the favour I expect from your ladyship, I will here, before God Almighty, really and freely promise how things is. First, that this is the last time I shall trouble your ladyship or any of my friends in Scotland. Secondly, I do here promise faithfully that as soon as I come to Spain, with all possible haste that can be, out of the first moneys I am to receive there (where I am to receive reasonable store) I shall hasten those moneys to Scotland to your ladyship or my Lord of Rothes or Kinghorn with all the haste that can be imagined. Yet I know my moneys cannot come in time from Spain to pay those moneys I take here presently at the day appointed, the failing of which will be my utter ruine and disgrace here and in Spain.

Therefore, madam, for the love of God, and as ever you will think me worthy of the title of your son, fail me not at this time. I have written to my Lord of Rothes and Kinghorn to this same etect, who, I hope, will join with you for the lifting of those moneys only for one term, and I protest to God I shall have money at you before the next. So, dear madam, let me once again on my knees beg this favour of you, and I protest to God I shall perform all I have promised your ladyship, how the doing the business or the not doing it is the ruining or making my fortune; and so I pray you to convey it, for I protest to God it is so, for if were with you that I might say which I dare not writ3. I know I nsed not fear the granting my desire. I shall say no more at this time, only I pray to God to bless you and all your company; so I humbly rest, your ladyship's most faithful son and humble servant, Buchan.

P. S. I cannot as yet write how much money I shall take up here, but I think it will be ten or twelve thousand marks."

The following letter, written by Marie, Countess of Buclian, shortly before her death, is of a singularly pathetic character. It is remarkable also for being signed by her maiden name:

"From Marie, Countess of Buchan, to the Countess of Mar.

London, 1628.

Dear Madame, Since I am almost past hope ever to see your ladyship, or ever to have the occasion offered which I coidd have wished to have shown my thankfulness for your ladyship's many great favours towards me, I am forced to write you now, having little or no further time to show my desires. For I having found your ladyship's kindness and help to be great in all which concerned me, I must now, in my greatest necessity, beg your prayers for me that I may ever continue more beholden to your ladyship than to anyone else. I am certain I need not recommend my greatest worldly care to your ladyship, which is the welfare and education of my children, for I have ever found your motherly affection towards me and them, that I persuade myself that they shall never want a loving mother as long as it shall please God to preserve your ladyship to them. I have no desire more earnest, which I shall still pray and wish for to my last, having it in the very greatest regrets that I cannot have the contentment to see your ladyship, yet I cannot be deprived of having my best wishes to your ladyship, which none shall go further in than I, who ever is your most affectionate and obedient daughter, Marie Douglas."

The Countess died in 1628, and the Earl in 1640. The latter died in London, and was buried within Auchterhouse Church. On the death of the Countess Marie, her estates passed to her son instead of her husband, for reasons that are obvious from the peculiarly sad tone of her correspondence, and the character of the Earl. Their son, James, who succeeded to the estates and title was a devoted Koyalist. He was present at the meetings of the Scottish Parliament in 1 641, which the King attended personally, and at which he employed his diplomacy in endeavouring to win over the other Covenanting Lords, as he had enlisted the services of Montrose. He was also present when the sentence of forfaultrey was pronounced against Montrose and the Ogilvies, and subsequently shared in other important parliamentary transactions. For some time he appears to have acted with the Covenanters; but, ultimately, on the breaking up of the party, became an opponent of the policy of Argyll. He was one of the Scottish nobles strongly opposed to the delivering up of the King by the Covenanters in 1646. In 1648 he was also one of the most active promoters of the Engagement, to which he dedicated his sword, energies, and fortune, and raised a considerable number of troojiters within the parish, and with them marched into England with the Scottish army, under the Duke of Hamilton, to attempt the release of the King, then a prisoner in the Isle of Wight. This army was defeated disastrously by Cromwell at the battle of Preston, and several of the Auchterhouse troopers perished in the battle and retreat. For his strong royalist partisanship, malignant tendencies, contempt for the Solemn League and Covenant, and his position as promoter of the ill-fated Engagement, he brought down upon himself the censure of the Church, and came frequently into collision with the ecclesiastical authorities within the parish, as will be afterwards shown, when we refer to the parochial records of this century. The Earl was visited at Auchterhouse by the young King, afterwards Charles II., on a somewhat remarkable occasion. The Prince being in the hands of the Presbyterian party, endeavoured to make his escape from their over-stern and irksome guardianship. He entertained the idea of putting himself at the head of a numerous body of Royalists in the North. Accordingly, under the pretext of hawking, he left Perth in semi-disguise on the 4th October 1650, accompanied by five of his servants. To avoid suspicion, he rode through the South Inch at a slow rate, but as soon as he cleared it he proceeded at full gallop to Dudhope Castle, Dundee. Along with Viscount Dudhope he proceeded to Auchterhouse, where he was received by Lord Buchan. The party then continued north to Cortachy Castle, the residence of the Earl of Airlie. The anticipated rising of the loyal clans proved a fiasco. From Cortachy Castle he was conducted by a Highland escort for security to Clova, where he was discovered by a body of troopers who had been despatched from Perth in pursuit, and with strict orders to bring him back. The troopers found him " lying in a filthy room on an old bolster, above a matt of sedges and rushes, and very fearful." He was conducted to the Presbyterian camp at Perth, where he arrived on a Sunday morning, fortunately just in time to hear " ane comfortable sermon." Doubtless, a few more lectures and sermons followed in rapid succession, for the Presbyterian preachers found it necessary to bestow on the King daily exhortations of alarming length, and of a mercilessly scathing and pungent character. Thus terminated the ludicrous escapade of the " Start."

When General Monk appeared before Dundee, for its fidelity to the Monarchy he despatched bodies of cavalry to scour the surrounding country to seize and bring in as prisoners all the recalcitrant Royalists. Most of the nobles and gentry, however, had already sought shelter within the walls of the town, and took part in its gallant but fruitless defence. Buchan and other members of the nobility were taken prisoners by Monk, and the Earl was afterwards fined 1,000 sterling by Cromwell for his Monarchical sympathies. After the Restoration, the Earl was present as one of the chief mourners at the re-interment of the remains of the great Marquis of Montrose. After the execution of the latter, according to the barbarous practice of the age, his body was dismembered, and portions of it distributed in different parts of the country. These remains were recovered, and lay in state in the Abbey Church of Holyrood from 7th January to 11th May 1661. The public ceremonial of the "true funeralls" was afterwards conducted with great heraldic pomp and splendour.

The Earl's sister, Lady Elizabeth Erskine, who was married to the nephew of Montrose, Archibald, Second Lord Napier, rendered herself somewhat of a heroine by procuring the heart of Montrose immediately after his execution. She had it carefully embalmed, and it was long preserved in a gold filagree box,, and esteemed as a sacred relic by her family. Montrose had promised to leave her his heart as a mark of his affection for her, and in return for the unremitting kindness she had shown to him throughout the manifold vicissitudes of his life and fortune.

James, Earl of Buchan, married Lady Marjory, daughter of William Ramsay, First Earl of Dalhousie, a lady who subsequently figured in a very unpleasant position before the congregation of Auchterhouse Church. James, Ninth Earl, died in 1664. He left one son and five daughters.

In all probability, the turreted residence which succeeded the old castle of the Ramsays was at this time extended, and the house rearranged after the baronial st de of architecture. From its present appearance, there can be no doubt that the house has been erected at different periods. Although the walls are very thick and strong, still the buildingwas never adapted for defensive purposes. There is nothing remarkable about the exterior of the building. It is exceedingly plain but substantial. The original entrance to the house was by a small but massive door in the tower. This door with its quaint and guarded look-out holes has been reproduced, and is still maintained. The door leads to a very old and curious crypt-shaped apartment. This was protected by another strong door at one time, as was often the case where the crypt-shaped old halls existed. The original access to the upper rooms was by a spiral stair, part of which may still be seen behind the old doorway. While the exterior of the building is plain and unpretentious, the interior is of much interest. The finest room in the house is the present drawing-room, which, in former times, was used as the hall.

The initials, I. E. B. and C. M. B., appear on the finely-ornamented chimney-piece and in monogram upon the elaborately-decorated stucco ceiling. The arms are those of Buchan. The monogram rea ds James. Earl of Buchan, and Countess Marjory Buchan. The mouldings, cornices, tracery, and beautiful pendants, from their highly-finished character, are fine examples of that ornate design characteristic of the Jacobean period. This beautiful ceiling has been reproduced in the drawing-room of Cortachy Castle. There are also some interesting specimens of old tracery and richly-decorated work in other portions of the house.

William, who became Eighth Earl, joined in the wars of the Kevolution, and fought gallantly at the battle of Killiecrankie. He was one of the officers who attended upon the great Dundee when he succumbed to his wounds in the hour of victory. By the forces of King William he was subsequently made prisoner, and died within the walls of Stirling Castle. Having died unmarried, the title passed in 1695 to David Erskine, Fourth Lord Cardross, in virtue of which the title of Lord Auchterhouse is still hsld by the present representative of the ancient dignity. Nearly all the possessions in this parish, so long held by this historical family, passed out of their hands about 1620, although they still continued to reside, as Ave have shown, within the mansiondiouse, and held some of the adjacent property.

About 1G20, the Earl of Moray, through his grandfather, was retoured in lands of Auchterhouse and others. On 15th June 1648, Patrick, Earl of Kinghorne, was retoured in half of the lands and barony of Auchterhouse, which he had acquired. On the 12th May 1663, George, Earl Pannmre, held the same lands. Shortly after this they were for some time in possession of the Dalziel family, in the person of the Earl of Carnwath. On 2nd June 1621, considerable portions of the estates were in the possession of Lady Xevay, wife of Lord John Hay of Murie. On 29th October 1695, John, Earl of Strathmore, was retoured in the land-; of Auchterhouse, including the teinds of the rectory and vicarage of the parish. By the Earl of Strathmore they were granted to his second son, the Hon. Patrick Lyon. Ochterlony, who wrote in 1684, says " Ochterhouse, for the most part, belongs to the Earl of Strathmore. There is a fine house, good yards, excellent pastures and meadows, with a dovecot." At this time the house was considered to be one of the best examples of the old plain substantial Scottish baronial residences in this part of the country. When the Hon. Patrick Lyon became proprietor, he took up his residence within the mansiondiouse. He married a daughter of Mr Carnegie of Findhaven, and their initials, P. L. and M. C., may be seen cut out on a stone in front of the house. Patrick Lyon was Member for the County from 1703 to 1707. His name frequently occurs in the history of the Pebellion of 1715, and he was one of those who signed the proclamation in favour of the Pretender, the Chevalier de St George, the eldest son of James VII. With all their characteristic genuine affection for the Stewarts, the

Strathmore family espoused the cause of the Pretender. On his way to the so-called Coronation scene at Scone, he and his-suite were received and entertained with royal honours at Glamis Castle. The Strathmore family, indeed, were among the-chief promoters of the rising against the Hanoverian succession. With all the ardour of the old Jacobite, Lyon accordingly joined the rebel army under the Earl of Mar, who had unfurled the standard of the Chevalier at Braemar, on the 6th September 1715. To him as to others in Angus it proved a disastrous movement, as he was killed with his nephew, the young Earl of Strathmore, at the battle of Sherriffmuir

"Strathmore and Clanronald Cry'd still ' Advance, Donald," Till both of these heroes did fa', man; For there was such hashing, And broadswords a' clashing, Brave Forfar himself got a claw, man; And we ran, and they ran, c."

On the 9th May 1628, Patrick Lyon's other nephew, who became Earl of Strathmore, was mortally wounded in a sad affray at Forfar. Mr Carnegie of Lour, on the occasion of his daughter's funeral, entertained the Earl of Strathmore, his own brother James Carnegie of Findhaven, Lyon of Brigton, and others. After the ceremony they all adjourned to a tavern, and according to the foolish custom of the times, indulged too freely. Lyon, in the course of conversation, made some offensive observations about his sister-in-law, the Lady of Auchterhousc, and also grossly insulted Carnegie. In the evening the party sallied forth in a highly-excited condition, whereupon Lyon pushed Carnegie into a ditch. Carnegie at once drew his sword, ran at Lyon, and while Strathmore interposed he received a wound which terminated fatally. Carnegie was tried for manslaughter but acquitted. He also incurred the opprobrium of the Jacobites for his alleged base desertion of their cause, of Avhich he professed at one time to be a strong partisan. It was openly asserted that he had been bought over to the Hanoverian party by liberal bribes. Such conduct naturally created a bitter animus against him, and rendered him the sport of the clever but merciless Jacobite satirists. In a very quaint old song, entitled " He winna be guidit by me," Carnegie is thus held up to scorn and ridicule:

"0, heavens, he's ill to be guidit, His colleagues and he are dividit, Wi' the Court of Hanover he's sidit He winna be guidit by me.

They ca'd him their joy and their darling, Till he took their penny of arling; But he'll prove as false as Macfarlane He winna be guidit by me.

He was brought South by a merling, Got a hundred and fifty pounds sterling, Which will make him bestow the auld carlin' He winna be guidit by me.

He's angered his goodson and Fintry, By selling his King and his country, And put a deep stain on the gentry He'll never be guidit by me.

He's joined the rebellious club, too, That endeavours our peace to disturb, too, He's cheated poor Mr John Grub, too, And he's guilty of simony.

He broke his promise before, too, To Fintry, Auchterhouse, and Strathmore, too; God send him a heavy glengore, too For that is the death he will die."

Shortly after Patrick Lyon's death the lands of Auchterhouse were acquired by John, Fourth Earl of Airlie. The noble family of Airlie, so long connected with this parish, is descended from Gilbert, the third son of the first Thane of Angus, a gentleman of much distinction in the reign of William the " Lion." He fought at the battle of the Standard in 1138. Subsequently, he obtained charters from William of the lands of Powrie, Ogilvy, and Lintrathen, and took the name of Ogilvy from his barony in the parish of Glamis. From him was descended Sir "Walter Ogilvie, who married the heiress of Auchterhouse, to whom we have already referred. Descended from him was Sir James Ogilvy, who was so highly esteemed by King James IV. that he was created a Peer, with the title of Oo-ilvie of Airlie, and sat in Parliament in 1491. He held for some time the post of Ambassador from Scotland to the Court of Denmark.

The Seventh Lord Ogilvy, in return for his services to King Charles I., and for his repeated acts of loyalty, was created Earl of Airlie in 1639. During his flight into England, to escape the signing of the Solemn League and Covenant, and the rancorous hostility of Argyll, his Castle of Airlie, and that of Forthour, in Glenisla, were destroyed by fire and completely dismantled by the forces of the Covenant, acting under the command of the Marquis. The incident has been very finely depicted in one of the most expressive and graceful of the Scottish ballads:

"It fell on a day, a bonnie summer day,
When the leaves were green and yellow; That there fell out a great dispute Between Argyll and Airly.
Argyll lias ta'en a hunder o' his men,
A hunder men and mairly; And he's away by the back o' Dunkeld
To plunder the bonnie hoose o' Airly.
The lady looked o'er the hie Castle wa',
And, oh! but she sighed sairly When she saw Argyll and a' his men
Come to plunder the bonnie hoose o' Airly.
Clouds o' smoke and flames sae blue Soon left the walls but barely,
And she laid her doun on that hill to die, When she saw the burnin' o' Airly."

Lord Ogilvie, the eldest son of the Earl of Airlie, became intimately associated with Montrose when the latter abandoned the cause of the Covenanters. So deeply had he offended the Presbyterian leaders, that a reward of one thousand pounds was offered for his capture. Subsequently, we find him accompanying Montrose, who, at the head of a fine body of Scottish cavalry six thousand strong, marched into England to reinforce the Eoyal army, now hard pressed by Cromwell. The unfortunate defeat, through the rashness of Prince Eupert at Marston Moor which took place the day previous to the anticipated meeting between the Scots and the Koyal forces completely upset the plans of Montrose. Greatly disappointed with the failure of the expedition and the Eoyal reverse, he withdrew his cavalry to Carlisle. Lord Ogilvie at this time appears to have been recognised as a shrewd and able officer by his Chief. He was ordered by Montrose to proceed from Carlisle into Scotland to ascertain the movements of the Covenanters a hazardous journey which he, however, successfully accomplished in disguise, although the report with which he returned: that the whole country was in the hands of Argyll, had b ' no means an exhilarating effect upon his commander. He was next despatched as a special envoy by Montrose to the South, to represent the serious position of affairs personally to the King, and to urge him to hasten supplies of men and arms to enable him to open the Scottish campaign with some prospect of success. On his way South, however, with a small detachment of cavalry, Lord Ogilvie was attacked and defeated by one of Cromwell's officers, and made prisoner. Placed under guard, he was sent to Hull, thence to Edinburgh, where he was thrown into prison, and remained there for about a year, until released by the orders of Montrose after his victory at Kilsyth. When Montrose crossed the Scottish border, and had succeeded by his indomitable energy and great tact in raising in his favour the loyal clans, the Earl of Airlie, although well-advanced in years and by no means in the best of health, entered enthusi- astically into his service, and by him was esteemed as a warm personal friend and a brave and accomplished soldier. Personal quite as much as political influences led him to take the field against his old enemy, Argyll. Proceeding northwards, they defeated the Campbells at Inverlochy, in which engagement, however, Airlie lost his son, Sir Thomas, who was mortally wounded, to the great grief of Montrose. This promising osicer, to whom Montrose greatly owed his victory, was buried with full military honours in Athole. Bishop Wishart refers to him in the following eulogistic terms: " From the beginning of the Scots war he had adhered closely to Montrose, by whom he was in a particular manner beloved. Besides his reputation in a military capacity, he was likewise well versed in the sciences, and was in every respect an additional honour and grace to the ancient family of the Ogilvies. As he was a main instrument in obtaining the victory, his death was answerable to the great character he had acquired, thus falling in the defence of his King and country." In a letter written by Montrose to King Charles L, dated February 1645, he mentions that Sir Thomas had been severely and dangerously wounded. " Your Majesty had never a truer servant, nor there never was a truer, honester man." It was, however, at the battle of Kilsyth that Lord Airlie particularly distinguished himself. When the battle was apparently going in favour of the Covenanting army through the imprudence and impetuosity of the Highlanders of the clans M'Gregor and M'Lean, who, under their brave but impulsive chiefs, made a wild onslaught upon the Presbyterian cavalry and infantry contrary to the orders of Montrose, and unsupported by the other divisions of the army; Montrose at once perceived that his forces would soon be overwhelmed by the numerical superiority of the Covenanters. Riding up to Airlie, who was at the head of his troopers, the Ogilvies, and apparently somewhat indignant at being left out of the fight, Montrose thus addressed him " You see, my Lord, what a hose net those poor fellows have got themselves into by their ill-advised daring. They must certainly he trampled in the dirt hy the enemy's horse if not speedily relieved. I venture to apply to your Lordship for this purpose, hecause the eyes of all the officers are fixed upon you as alone worthy of such a piece of precedency, and hecause it seems proper that an error which has been committed by the foolhardiness of youth should be corrected by the veteran discretion and considerable valour of so venerable a warrior as your Lordship. Forward! in the name of God, and show these mad lads that, clever as they think themselves, they may still be beholden occasionally to older men than themselves." Airlie, at the head of his horsemen, at once charged, and with so much success that fortune turned in favour of the Royalists, and Kilsyth was won. In this battle it was alleged that 6,000 Covenanters fell. This was the most im-portant of the victories obtained by Montrose, and made him for the time supreme in Scotland. Lord Airlie and his son, Lord Ogilvie, were also present at the disastrous battle of Philliphaugh 13th September 1645), which practically closed the military career of the great Marquis. Airlie only escaped with his Chief and other officers by hard riding from the battlefield. His son, Lord Ogilvie, who acted as aide-de-camp to Montrose, was taken prisoner having lost his way in the retreat and afterwards condemned to be beheaded at the Cross of St Andrews. The night before his execution, however, he was very cleverly rescued from the Castle of St Andrews. His sister, Helen Ogilvie, wife of Sir John Carnegie, together with his mother and wife, through the influence of Lindsay and Hamilton, succeeded in obtaining what was believed to be the final interview with him.

When they entered his prison, Lord Ogilvie was in bed feigning very serious illness. The guards from compassion having temporarily withdrawn, Ogilvie disguised himself with his sister's dress, and concealed his features with her long robe and hood. When the guards returned, they found the pretended invalid as they left him; but who was none other than his devoted sister, who had put on his nightcap and taken her brother's place in bed. The final interview was thus concluded, and, holding their handkerchiefs to their faces as if overwhelmed with grief, the party was conducted under torchlight from the sloom of the dungeon and without the castle walls. Horses being in readiness not far off, all escaped safely. Ogilvie, however, found it necessary to leave the country for Trance as quickly as possible. Argyll Avas so enraged at his escape that it required all the influence of the Hamiltons to protect the lives of those who had shared in the artful and daring stratagem. The members of the family implicated were ordained " to be sett at libertie, each of them finding surety for their behaviour and compirance for 1,000 lib. a pice."

Notwithstanding the granting of an amnesty by General David Lesly to all who had taken up arms, Lord Ogilvie joined in the rising under Mackenzie of Pluscarden. This was denounced as an unnatural war, " as the tearing of the bowells of their awen native country." In spite of all appeals and remonstrances, he continued to defy the Covenanters. At a meeting of the Scottish Parliament held in 1649, " a Committee tampered a quhyle with the Lord Ogilvey, he being remitted by the Generall Assembly to them, bot could prevaill nothing with him to conforme himselve to the Acte of the Generall Assembly, so that they gave him the 1 day of November nixt, ather to give satisfactione, utherwayes they assured him that then and no longer the Church wolde superseed the pronouncing sentence of excommunication against him for his contumacy and disobedience." In spite of all their anathemas he remained a confirmed irreconcilable. Lord Airlie continued, like his son, unswerving to the last in his allegiance to the Royalist policy, and a staunch friend and companion-in-arms of the unfortunate Marquis. In a letter written by the King to Montrose he refers to Lord Airlie and others in those terms: " Whenever God shall enable me they shall reap the fruits of their loyalty and affection to my service." Ochterlony (1684-5) thus refers to the distinction won by the Airlie family: " The family is very ancient and honourable, and have been ever famous for their loyaltie, especialle in the times of our civill warrs. The late and present Earl of Airlie, with Sir Thomas, who died in the Prince's service, and Sir David, now living, have, with diverse others of their name, given such evident testi-mounie of their loyaltie to their Prince that will make them famouse to all succeeding generations; Avhich, doubtless, you will get account of to be recorded to their everlasting honour."

During the occupation of Scotland by Cromwell the Airlie lands were forfeited; but by order of the Commissioners of Confiscated Estates, Lady Helen Ogilvie, widow of the late Earl, was permitted to receive one-fifth of the rents of the lands.

James, the Second Earl, who fled to France after his escape from prison, appears to have returned during the Commonwealth, with whose Head he had the prudence to remain at peace. At the Restoration he was made a Privy Councillor, and served as an officer in the royal service.

In 1677, when King Charles II. found it necessary to raise three independent troops of horsemen to assist in quelling the disturbances in Scotland, he appointed Claverhouse to the command of the first. The other commissions were conferred upon Lord Airlie and Lord Home by Lauderdale. Lord Airlie took part in the invasion of the western counties by the Highland host, and had some share in the cruel suppression of the Covenanters. When, by orders of King James, Claverhouse inarched with the Scottish cavalry to England, he was joined at Cambridge by the soldier chief of the Ogilvies, who proved himself, notwithstanding his age, as efficient an officer as ever. He was subsequently placed in command of the Scottish bodyguard which escorted the King to the army at Salisbury. This dashing cavalier was succeeded by his son David, who became Earl of Airlie. This Earl had two sons, James and John. James, Lord Ogilvy, having thrown himself into the ill-fated

Rebellion of 1715, and fought at Sherifftnuir, was attainted of high treason; but his estate was saved by being in his father's name, who was still alive. He was afterwards pardoned. As James, Lord Ogilvy, died without issue, he was succeeded by his brother John, the Fourth Earl of Airlie, who purchased the Auchterhouse estates. His son David, Lord Ogilvie afterwards Fifth Earl of Airlie was one of the most devoted of the Jacobites, and joined the rebel army at Edinburgh under "Bonnie Prince Charlie" in 1745, with 600 men, principally drawn from his own clan and estates. That such a large body of men should have been raised for the most part from the Airlie estates may be accounted for from the fact, that the Earl issued strict orders to all his tenants, ground officers, and dependants upon the estates to take up arms. Yery many of them were thus forced to accompany Lord Ogilvie; although the Earl himself very cautiously, and fortunately, as events transpired, took great care not to identify himself too openly with the Rebellion. This fine body of men proved an important accession to the Highland army. Ogilvie joined the Prince in Edinburgh after the battle of Prestonpans in 1745, where the Royalist forces were completely overpowered by the fierce onslaught of the stalwart Highlanders. He joined in the victorious march over the border, and afterwards fought at Culloden in 1746, where the Jacobite army suffered irretrievable defeat. Fleeing from the battlefield, he made his escape to Dundee, thence to Norway, where he was made prisoner. He escaped to Sweden, thence to France, and there became an officer in the French service. The unswerving devotion and self-sacrifice which this young but undaunted Jacobite soldier displayed to have the " auld Stewarts back again," although worthy of a nobler cause, nevertheless cannot fail to strike the imagination and evoke the warmest sympathies. Many a day the gallant Ogilvies, who survived Drummossie Muir, and the savage reprisals which followed, lamented the absence of their chief an exile in foreign lands for whom they entertained the fondest regard, and from whom to be separated was the most bitter disappointment of their lives.

"Over the seas and far awa', Over the seas and far awa', 0, weel may we maen for the day that's gane, And the lad that's banished far awa'.

The following entry appears in the parochial baptismal records of this period: "December 6, 1751, which day David Ogilvie, lawful son to the Eight Hon. David, Lord Ogilvy, and Lady Margaret Johnstone, his spouse, and grandson to the Right Hon. John, Earl of Airlie, residing at Auchterhouse, was baptysed in the presence of several persons of distinction." Having obtained a free pardon, the Earl returned to Scotland in 1783, and died, after a strangely romantic and chequered career, in 1803. His sword and drinking cup his companions throughout many years of struggle, hardship, and exile for the Stewart cause are still preserved at Cortachy Castle. Inscribed upon the sword are the interesting words " The man who feels no delight in a gallant steed, a bright sword, and a fair lady has not in his breast the heart to be a soldier." Upon the cup are inscribed the family arms, and words very expressive of the owner's vicissitudes of fortune " If fortune torments me, hope contents me." The Countess of Airlie, a daughter of Sir James Johnstone of "Westerhall, equalled her husband in her devotion to the Jacobite cause; for, accompanying the Highland army, she witnessed the fight at Culloden. There she was taken prisoner and removed to Edinburgh Castle. She, however, cleverly managed to make her escape from the Castle to France, where she died in exile in the year 1757, at the early age of thirty-three. Walter Ogilvy of Airlie assumed the title of Lord Airlie in 1812. The title, however, was for some time in abeyance, and was not restored till the year 1826. Although portions of the Auchterhouse estate have within recent years been sold, the old mansion-house, with the adjoining lands, still remains in the possession of the present Earl of Airlie.

From the fact that the tower and manor-house were for so many years occupied by the Earls of Buchan, a large saugh tree within the grounds is understood to mark the spot where, it is alleged, the fight so renowned in Scottish ballad took place between Sir John de Graeme and Sir James the Eoss or Rose for the hand of the fair Matilda, the daughter of one of the Earls of Buchan. The old ballad of Sir James the Rose was at one time a very familiar one throughout Scotland. From the original ballad have sprung other two, viz., "Sir James the Ross," and " Sir James of Perth." The following, however, is the ballad which we have frequently heard quoted throughout the parish. It is an interesting and spirited production, understood to be from the pen of Michael Bruce, although founded upon the earlier versions:

SIR JAMES THE ROSE.

Of all the Scottish Northern chiefs,
Of high and warlike name, The bravest was Sir James the Rose,
A knight of meikle fame.
His growth was like the youthful oak
That crowns the mountain's brow, And waving o'er his shoulders broad
His locks of yellow new.
Wide were his fields, his herds were large,
And large his flocks of sheep, And numerous were his goats and deer,
Upon the mountains steep.
The chieftain of the good clan Rose,
A firm and warlike band, Five hundred warriors drew the sword,
Beneath his high command.
In bloody fight thrice had he stood
Against the English keen, Ere two-and-twenty opening springs
The blooming youth had seen.
The fair Matilda dear he loved
A maid of beauty rare; Ev'n Margaret on the Scottish throne
Was never half so fair.
Long had he woo'd, long she refused,
With seeming scorn and pride; Yet oft her eyes confessed the love
Her fearful words denied.
At length she blessed his well-tried love,
Allowed his tender claim; She vowed to him her tender heart,
And owned an equal flame.
Her father, Buchan's cruel lord,
Their passion disapproved; He bade her wed Sir John the Gramme,
And leave the youth she loved.
One night they met as they were wont,
Deep in a shady wood, Y here on the bank beside the burn
A blooming saugh tree stood.
Concealed among the underwood
The crafty Donald lay The brother of Sir John the Grseme
To watch what they might say.
"When thus the maid began, My Sire
Our passion disapproves, He bids me wed Sir John the Gra? me,
So here must end our loves.
My father's will must be obeyed,
Nought boots me to withstand; Some fairer maid in beauty's bloom

Shall bless you with her hand.
Soon will Matilda be forgot,
And from thy mind effaced; But may that happiness be thine,
Which I can never taste.
What do I hear! is this thy vow?
Sir James the Rose replied; And will Matilda wed the Graeme,
Though sworn to be my bride?
His sword shall sooner pierce my heart Than 'reave me of thy charms
And clasped her to his throbbing breast, Fast locked within his arms.
I spoke to try tliy love, she said, I'll ne'er wed man but thee;
The grave shall be my bridal bed If Grseme my husband be.
Then take, dear youth, this faithful kiss
In witness of my troth, And every plague become my lot,
That day I break my oath:
They parted thus the sun was set
Up hasty Donald flies, And turn thee, turn thee, beardless youth,
He loud insulting cries.
Soon turned about the fearless chief, And soon his sword he drew;
For Donald's blade before his breast Had pierced his tartans through.
This for my brother's slighted love, His wrongs sit on my arm
Three paces back the youth retired, To save himself from harm.
Returning swift his sword he reared, Fierce Donald's head above;
And through the brain and crashing bone His furious weapon drove.
Life issued at the wound he fell
A lump of lifeless clay; So fall my foes, quoth valiant Rose,
And stately strode away.
Thro' the green wood in haste he passed,
Unto Lord Buchan's hall, Beneath Matilda's window stood,
And thus on her did call:
Art thou asleep, Matilda dear?
Awake, my love, awake; Behold thy lover waits without
A long farewell to take.
For I have slain fierce Donald Grseme,
His blood is on my sword; And far, far distant are my men,
Nor can defend their lord.
To Skye I will direct my flight
Where my brave brothers bide, To raise the mighty of the Isles,
To combat on my side.
0 do not so, the maid replied,
With me till morning stay; For dark and dreary is the night,
And dangerous is the way.
All night I'll watch thee in the park,
My faithful page I'll send In haste to raise the brave clan Rose
Their master to defend.
He laid him down beneath a bush

And wrapped him in his plaid; While trembling for her lover's fate
At distance stood the maid.
Swift ran the page o'er hill and dell,
Till in a lowly glen He met the furious Sir John Graeme,
With twenty of his men.
Where goest thou, little page, he said,
So late? who did thee send? I go to raise the brave clan Rose,
Their master to defend.
For he has slain fierce Donald Graeme,
His blood is on his sword, And far, far distant are his men,
Nor can assist their lord.
And has he slain my brother dear?
The furious chief replies; Dishonour blast my name but he
By me ere morning dies.
Say, page, where is Sir James the Rose?
I will thee well reward He sleeps into Lord Buchans park,
Matilda is his guard.
They spurred their steeds and furious fle. v
Like lightning o'er the lea; They reached Lord Buchan's lofty tower
By dawning of the day.
Matilda stood withoiit the gate
Upon a rising ground, And watched each object in the dawn,
All ear to every sound.
Where sleeps the Bose? began the Graeme,
Or lias the felon fled? This hand shall lay the wretch on earth,
By whom my brother bled.
Last day at noon, Matilda said, Sir James the Rose passed by,
Well mounted on his noble steed, And onward fast did hie.
By this time he's in Edinburgh Town, If horse and man hold good;
Your page then lied, who said he was Now sleeping in the wood.
She wrung her hands and tore her hair;
Brave Rose, thou art betrayed, And ruined by the very means
From whence I hoped thine aid.
And now the valiant knight awoke,
The virgin shrieking heard; Straight up he rose and drew his sword
When the fierce band appeared.
Your sword last night my brother slew,
His blood yet dims its shine; And ere the sun shall gild the morn,
Your blood shall reek on mine.
Your words are brave, the chief returned,
But deeds approve the man, Set by your men, and hand-to-hand
We'll try what valour can.
With dauntless step he forward strode,
And dared him to the fight; The Graeme gave back, he feared his arm,
For well he knew his might.

Four of his men, the bravest four,
Sunk down beneath his sword; But still he scorned the poor revenge,
And sought their haughty lord.
Behind him basely came the Graeme,
And pierced him in the side; Out sprouting came the purple stream,
And all his tartans dyed.
But yet his hand dropped not the sword,
Nor sunk he to the ground, Till through his enemy's heart the steel
Had forced a mortal wound.
Graeme, like a tree by wind o'erthrown,
Fell breathless on the clay; And down beside him sunk the Rose,
And faint and dying lay.
Matilda saw and fast she ran, 0 spare his life, she cried; Lord Buchan's daughter begs his life,
Let her not be denied.
Her well-known voice the hero heard, And raised his death-closed eyes;
He fixed them on the weeping maid, And weakly thus replies:
In vain l. latilda begs a life By death's arrest denied;
My race is run adieu, my love; Then closed his eyes and died.
The sword yet warm from his left side With frantic hand she drew;
I come, Sir James the Rose, she cried, I come to follow you.
The hilt she leant against the ground, And bared her snowy breast,
Then fell upon her lover's face, And sunk to endless rest.

There is considerable historical interest also attached to the lands of DronlaaV, which lie within the parish. These lands at a very remote period formed a portion of the extensive estates of the Earls of Mar, whose descendants subsequently held. the Barony of Anchterhouse. About the year 1251, the Earl of Mar bestowed the lands of Dronlaw upon a representative of a well-known Scottish family, the Hays of Errol, a grant which was afterwards confirmed by Donald, Earl of Mar, between 1272 and 1294. In a charter, dated at Lindores, 1st August 1294, King John Baliol granted certain lands, in which Dronlaw was included, to Nicolas de Hay of Errol. In 1296, Sir John de la Hay of Angus, the proprietor of Dronlaw, was one of the Barons who swore fealty to King Edward I. Sir Gilbert de Hay, the oldest son of Nicolas, was one of the knights who took the side of Bruce when he ascended the throne in March 1306, and remained his adherent throughout his early adventurous career. By the chronicles of the period he is designated the loyal Hay. The family war-cry " The Hay! The Hay!"

was one which frequently resounded over the battlefields of the early Scottish wars.

"The King had in hys cumpany James alsua of Douglas, That wycht, wyse and worthy was; Schyr Gilbert de la Hay alsua."'

When the King and his followers were on one occasion attacked by the men of Lorn, it is related that

"James off Douglas was hurt that tyd, And als Sir Gilbert de la Hay."

And again

"The King now takys hys gate to ga. And with hym tuk he sergeands tvva, And Schyr Gilbert de la Hay left he Thar for to rest with hys menye."

In return for his services he was created Constable of Scotland. He was one of the Scottish barons who signed the letter to the Pope asserting the independence of Scotland, 6th April 1320. He died in 1330, and was buried within the Abbey of Coupar. On the 6th May 1324, Sir Gilbert Hay made a grant in pure and perpetual alms to Almighty God and to the blessed Dominic, for the maintenance of one burning lamp and another burning lamp before the great cross in the Church of the Dominican Friars, Perth, to be paid half at the Feast of Pentecost, and the other half at the Feast of St Martin in the winter. Sir Gilbert was also a munificent bestower of grants to the Abbey of Coupar. Down to the middle of the 16th century the lands of Dronlaw remained in the Hay family. 29th Oct. 1546, John Scrymceour, the heir of James Scrymgeour, Constable of Dundee, was retoured in the lands of Dronlaw and Adainstone. On 17th April 1638, William Hay, heir of Sir Alexander Hay, was retoured in Dronlaw, c. On 30th August 1638, they passed to the Earl of Errol. 28th September 1652, George Hay was retoured in Dronlaw and other lands. In

Mr Robert Hay of Dronlaw acted as an elder in Auchterhouse Church. He is mentioned among the list of nobility and gentry preseirt at the re-interment of the great Marquis in 1661. His relative, Sir William Hay of Delgity, was a companion-in-arms of Montrose throughout his campaigns in Scotland. He accompanied him also during his flight, was made prisoner, and suffered death immediately after the execution of his chief. On the day of the re-interment of Montrose, his remains were laid beside those of his leader, amid all the honours which could be paid to a well-known cavalier and soldier of fortune.

The following inscription appears upon one of the present Communion Cups: " This Communion Cup, for the Kirk of Aughterhous, gifted be Mr Hay of Drolaw, and renewed Anno 1717." The original date of the cup is not given; probably it was gifted in the middle of the 17th century. The lands of Dronlaw were successively held by Lord Deskfruid (1652), Patrick Ogilvy (1671), Colin Campbell of Lundie (1670); then we find in 1695 that the Earl of Strathmore is retoured in lands of Dronlaw, Templeton, with the alehouse, manor, and teinds of the Church of Auchterhouse. They were afterwards acquired, along with the lands of Adamstone, by the family of Duncan, who owned the Templelands, in which family they still remain. The Templelands within the parish were so named because they originally formed a portion of the vast estates scattered over the country which belonged to the famous semi-religious order of Knight-Templars an order instituted in the 12th century for the defence of the Holy Sepulchre. Its wealth and landed possessions brought about its moral collapse, and ultimately the order was suppressed by Pope Clement V. These lands appear to have gradually passed into the hands of private individuals. In the 16th century, they were in the possession of William Duncan, whose descendants, represented by the Earl of Camper-down, are still in possession. The lands of Scotston within the parish formed at one time a portion of the valuable estates of the Earls of Angus.

ANGUS PARISH. (Jl
Part H.
THE CHURCH

There were no regular parochial priests in Scotland till the 12th century. In early times it was customary for wealthy barons to erect chapels upon their estates for the spiritual benefit of themselves and their retainers, and the land was then tithed for the maintenance of the priest. In these early times representatives of the various orders of monks from the monastic centres of Perth, Dundee, and other ecclesiastical establishments constantly traversed the country in all directions, and were, as a rule, liberally treated for their spiritual services. Scotland had now become a portion of the all-powerful and widespread territory of the Church of Eome. The clergy of that church soon acquired commanding influence, for they were the ouly educated men, the only legislators, and the only notaries, and even the proud barons acknowledged their authority. After this came a remarkable period in Scottish ecclesiastical history. Now originated its splendid hierarchy, and were erected its grand abbeys, churches, and chapels, which at the present day are still beautiful in their ruins. It was truly said of this time, that the sound of the gospel could scarcely be heard for the sound of the mallet. The energy displayed, even in the most remote districts, was unbounded in' its enthusiasm. Auchter-house, about this time, was created a vicarage in the Diocese of Dunkeld. When Galfridus was Bishop of Dunkeld in 1238, the Church of Utherhouse is mentioned as one of those under his jurisdiction. In the year 1275, Benimundus dc Vicci, better known as Bagimont, came to Scotland to collect on behalf of the Pope one-tenth of all ecclesiastical benefices for the recovery of the Holy Land. According to Bagimont's roll, made up at Perth in 1275, the vicarage was valued at 8 Scots, so that six centuries ago the parish possessed a Christian church and priest. In those days the old barons feared nothing on earth but the Church, and not one of them would have been bold enough to venture forth into the wars without its benediction. Besides, the stern uncompromising theology of Rome and the universal belief in the burning abyss where the departed had to expiate the sins which they had not expiated on earth, filled the minds of all in those dark, superstitious, and semi-barbarous times with indescribable terror. The wealthy feudal lords believed that whatever was spent upon a church would tend to secure the repose of the souls of their departed relatives; consequently, the wealth of the land simply poured into the capacious coffers of Rome.

Notwithstanding the unfortunate obscurity in which the parochial life of Scotland is involved during this period, still, from an examination of the Canons of the Church drawn up by the Provincial Councils held at Perth in 1242 and 1296, some interesting information maybe obtained. The Council of 1242 published certain canons under the authority of a bull of Pope Honorius III., which were ratified by the King and the Estates. These canons remained practically the law of the Romish Church in Scotland until its overthrow. The parish rectors and vicars were enjoined to wear the tonsure, to habilitate themselves in garments suitable to their position, and avoid such as were made of tartan and striped cloth; to lead pure, respectable, and honest lives; to adhere strictly to the celibate state (which, however, very few of the parochial clergy did); to abstain from all drunkenness and debauchery; to avoid inns, except of necessity and when on journeys. They were further enjoined not to interfere too much in secular matters; not to engage in worldly business, particularly if dishonest; to be diligent in their duties, offices, and studies; to celebrate studiously and devoutly, by day and night alike, their divine calling as God should enable them; to instruct the people diligently in the Articles of the Catholic Faith, and warn them to expound the same faith to their children; to maintain in good order the sacred establishment, and the vessels, vestments, books, and other articles connected with divine service; to be careful of all church property; to prevent all squandering of it, all thoughtless. giving of it away, and all unnecessary impoverishment of the parochial living.

Before the foundation of St Andrews in 1411, Scottish aspirants for the priesthood were educated at Paris and Oxford. The first Professorships at St Andrews were those of school divinity, philosophy, and logic. It was the only centre of intellectual activity in Scotland, and was the favourite training school for Scottish youth.

Churches were to be built of stone, and thereafter consecrated. They were also to be provided with befitting ornamentation, and all requisite ecclesiastical furniture, such as fonts, service books, c. No church or oratory was on any account to be constructed without the sanction of the Bishop. The rector or vicar was to be provided with a manse (mansio) suitable for the reception of a Bishop or Archbishop, for the maintenance of which he was to be held responsible. The stipend (sustentatio) was not to be less than ten merks sterling, and free from all burdens. The vicar was entitled to the tithes of corn, hay, wool, flax, milk, cheese, chickens, eggs, fish, garden fruits, c. Any attempt to defraud the vicar, or any refusal to give up the tithes at the proper time and in good condition, was to be followed by excommunication. The stigma of " Son of Perdition" was attached to anyone who attempted to be dishonest and disloyal to any churchman. It may be mentioned, also, that before 1232 a provincial council was held by a canon of which every parish priest was secured in the privilege of pasturing his cattle over the parish. From many regulations enjoined by these early canons, we may mention the following All parishioners after they have come to the years of discretion must confess their sins once a year to their own priest, or to another with his authority. They were required to be most faithful in receiving the sacraments, otherwise they might be driven from the church, and when dead be deprived of Christian burial. Everything connected with the administration and receiving of the sacraments must be done with all solemnity and order. No priest was allowed to join any persons in matrimony unless by proclamation of banns three times publicly in church according to the form of the General Council. No one dared, under the penalty of excommunication, to keep back any information which might prevent marriage, and no one was allowed to prevent a marriage maliciously. Clandestine marriages were strictly forbidden. Any priest being a party to such a marriage was liable to severe punishment. As the virtue and efficacy of the sacrament of baptism were held of the highest religious significance, it was ordained that it be celebrated with all honour, reverence, and care. A baptistry was to be provided for every church. The fonts were to be of stone or wood, and of sufficient size (competens). They were to be protected with covers (Fontes sub sera clausa custodian tur). Any breach of this order brought down upon the offender three months' suspension from office. The water in which a child shall have been baptised ought not be kept in the baptistry beyond seven days. After baptism the parents were very sensibly cautioned against allowing their children to go near fires and water. Churches were enjoined to be kept carefully both internally and externally. No filthy animals were allowed to run about at large in churchyards. Any unseemly behaviour in churches or churchyards, such as playing and dancing, was to be suppressed. Whoever was warned thrice by the parish priest and did not desist might be proceeded against. If this form of insolence continued, then excommunication was enjoined. Those fleeing to the churches for refuge should be defended.

except all such as were notorious highway robbers and violators of churches. When the priest is called to any sick person, and if after he has heard confession the person desire to make a will, the priest may advise him or induce him to remember the fabric of the cathedral, church, c.

The canons conclude as follows: " We excommunicate, condemn, anathematise, and we exclude from the Church of the holy mother of God, all conspirators against Prelates, Bishops, and Churchmen all abettors of such conspiracies all such as are heretical, schismatic, and infamous. We excommunicate all those who disturb the peace of the King and kingdom, all who for the sake of gain bring charges against others, by which their reputation is injured, and by whose evil actions death, exile, mutilation, and spoliations befall anyone. We excommunicate all defrauders of the tithes. highway robbers, plunderers of ecclesiastics, c. All such we proclaim accursed internally and externally, from the sole of the foot to the crown of the head. May their days be few, and may others receive their possessions. May their children be orphans. May their souls be plunged in hell, unless they repent and seek satisfaction and amendment. Fiat Fiat Amen."

Among the charters granted by King Robert III. between 1390 and 1-406 is one to Sir Alexander Ogilvie, Sheriff of Angus, of ten merks sterling, of the farm of the town of Nevay, in the barony of Eassie, to the foundation of ane chaplanrie in the kirk of Uchterhous. Subsequently, Sir Alexander made a grant of ten merks yearly of the lands of the Kirkton of Keillor and Eassie, and ten merks sterling out of Calcary, in Farnell. Gradually the endowments increased. There is a charter by King James I. confirming a charter by Sir Walter Ogilvie of Lintrathen, whereby he founds a chaplanrie within the Parish Church of St Mary, Auchterhouse, for two chaplains to perform service for the good estate of the King and Joanna Queen; and for the souls of the forefathers and successors of the King; and for the soul of the late Sir Walter Ogilvy, father of the granter, p and his mother; and for the soul of Isabel, his late spouse; and the souls of his brothers, forefathers, and successors; and the souls of those whom the said Sir Walter had offended, and to whom he had not made amends; as also for those who fell in the battle of Harlaw. He endows said chaplanrie with an annual pa unent of twenty merks. This charter is dated at Edinburgh, 28th January 1426. February 3, 1426, King James I. confirmed grant by Sir Walter de Ogilvie of Lintrathen of rents from Eassie, Keillor, and Calcary, to support two chaplains in the kirk of Auchterhouse. The chapel was dedicated to the Virgin, and called St Mary's. A skew-put stone, with the inscription " Ave Maria," and the fleur-dedis underneath, may still be seen built into the east gable of the present church. In the year 1426 the church or chapel gave place to a band-some edifice. This building was an extensive Gothic structure, and architecturally of some pretension. Gothic architecture was now in great perfection, richness, and variety. Sir Walter Ogilvie erected the chapel subseopicntly into a Provostry or College of Priests, Prebendaries, and Choristers. At this time very few monasteries were erected. Wealth and luxury had, to a large extent, rendered the monks of the period indolent and indifferent, and it was openly alleged that they even neglected to celebrate masses for the founders of their own establishments. A new religious foundation, therefore, became more fashionable amongst the nobles, viz., the Provostry or Collegiate Church, in which the secular canons or prebends formed a body occupied in the services of the church, and in celebrating masses for the founders.

What preaching there was wandered too frequently into the realm of the legendary and fabulous, and for many years this degradation of ministerial functions prevailed, until, as years rolled on, times utterly degenerate set in. Priests and people grew coarse in sentiment, in language, and in life, and going to chapel became little short of a mockery. Matters grew gradually worse. The clergy became shamefully dissolute and avaricious, and the people were simply robbed to maintain them.

The only prelate of any distinction in the 15th century was Bishop Kennedy. Lindsay says " He caused all parsons and vicars to remain at their parish churches for the instruction and edifying of their flocks, and caused them to preach the Word of God unto the people, and to visit them when they were sick; and also the said Bishop visited every church within his diocese four times in the year, and preached to the parishioners the Word of God truly, and enquired of them if they were duly instructed in the Word of God by their parson and vicar, and if their sacraments were duly administered, and if the poor were sustained, and the youth educated and taught conformably to the order that was taken in the Church of God. And where he found that order was not followed he made great punishment, to the effect that God's glory might shine through all the country within his diocese, giving good example to all future Archbishops and churchmen in general, to cause the patrimony of the Church of God to be used for the glory of God and the common benefit of the poor." The conduct of this venerable Bishop was most exceptional, as it was said of the Bishops in general that being shorn themselves they preached the shearing of their flocks with great assiduity and success.

The churches and religious houses in many places also appear to have lapsed into a state of wreck and decay. Prior to the Reformation the Privy Council issued a proclamation setting forth that they had understood that the i paroch kirks of this realm, partly by sloth and negligence of the parishioners, daily decay and became ruinous, and part of them are already fallen down, the parishioners noways causing the same to be mended; nor yet the parson doing what appertains to him for upholding thereof; also it is noticed that there lies bene diverse paroche kirkes within this realme demolished, casten down, and destroyed for the maist part, and that certaine particular persones has applyd the stanes, tymber, and uther greith perteining thereto to their awin particular use and profite. Although orders were issued to have them repaired and upbigged, to be mended in thack, and other necessaries, the complaint was general that the Act was not tane in na place because of the sleuth and unwillingness of the parishioners, quhilks were slaw and refused to chuse persones to tax their nichboures."

From the canons of 1549 we learn that in many populous parishes very many of the people had abandoned attendance upon Divine ordinances. Mass was seldom attended on Sundays, and festivals were much neglected. Those who did attend any of the services too often treated them with scoffing and contempt, whilst others turned the once highly-venerated place of worship into an ordinary rendezvous, and the church porch into a convenient place for the disjdOsal of merchandise. The church entirely got out of touch with the popular feeling. There was widespread indignation and dissatisfaction with the unmistakable corruption. The clergy grew more and more corrupt, and stubbornly blind to their real position. The utter collapse of the whole system became simply a question of time. In the midst of the unconcealed discontent, the news of that remarkable movement over the North Sea had spread abroad, and copies of Tyndale's New Testament, with the stirring pamphlets and sermons of the Reformers, were arriving at Dundee. The town soon openly renounced the doctrines of Rome, and won the reputation of being the first place of importance in Scotland to possess a church founded on the principles of the Reformed faith. Such men as "Wishart and the Wedderburns successively threw themselves zealously into the high enterprise of kindling the popular mind against the iniquities of the Church of Rome. Rousing preachers of the Reformed principles penetrated into the country districts, amongst whom none did better service than the eccentric but talented Paul Methven. A great change soon took place. The church, long a snare and delusion, was now a reproach. Priests and monks, friars and nuns, became the sport of the satirists, and the foibles of their lives were most mercilessly exposed. At length the order went forth: " Cut down the trees, and there will be no fear of the crows building." The monasteries and churches were at once attacked and levelled with the ground the ecclesiastical vestments, the chalices, the idols, and altars were consigned to the flames, and scarcely a vestige of the ancient superstition and idolatry was left.

"An' fearfu' the strarnash and stour, Whan pinnacle cam' down and tow'r; And Virgin Maries in a shower Fell flat and smash't their faces."

In 1567, such was the complete sweep made throughout Scotland, that all laws in favour of the Romish Church Avere repealed, the Protestant Confession of Faith was ratified and engrossed in the records, the saying of mass was declared to be a crime, the penalty being punishment and confiscation of goods for the first offence, banishment for the second, and death for the third.

In an age of unlimited superstition and credulity, there was ample opportunity for the creation of the mythical, weird, and romantic. The following account of an alleged case of cannibalism which occurred in this neighbourhood is illustrative of the age of monkish romances. The story is told by Pitscottie, although we can find no reference made to the circumstances by any other writer: "There was ane briggant ta'en with his hale familie, quho hauntit ane place in Angus. This mischievous man had an execrable faschion to tak' all young men or children aither he could steal away quietlie or tak' away without knowledge and ate them, and the younger they war esteemed them the more tender and delicious. For the whilk cause and dampnable abuse he with his wayff and bairns were all burnt, except ane young wench of ane year old, wha was saitfed and brought to Dundie, quhair she was broucht and fostered, and quhan shoe cam to ane voman's yeires she was condemned and burnt quick for that cryme. It was said that when shoe was coming to the place of execution thair gaithered ane nudge multitud of people, and speciallie of vonien, cursing her that shoe was so unhappy to committ sa damnable deides. To whom she turned about with an ireful cointenance, saying ' Quhairfira chyd yea me so as if I had committed an unworthy act? Give me credence and trow me; if yea had experience of eating men and vonien's flesh yac wad think it so delitious, that yea vould nevir forbear it agane." So, hot any signe of repentance, this unhappie traitour died in the sight of the people." The scene of this "Brigant's" cannibal operations was amongst the Sidlaws, and the Grlack of Newtyle was alleged to have been his chief rendezvous. It is a strange story, but too strange to be true. From the minuteness with which Pitscottie relates the story he seems to have accepted it as authentic throughout.

The first minister of the Eeformed Church of Scotland in this parish was the Rev. Alexander Tyrie, who was ordained in the memorable year 1567. He was translated to Meigle in 1572, but was re-appointed to this parish prior to 1582, with Tealing, Mains, and Strathmartine also under his charge. It is somewhat surprising to find one minister taking charge of four parishes; but the truth is, such a ministry was begun and spent in stormy times. Indeed, we can scarcely call it a ministry at all. War civil war furious and bloody, filled the land. The churches, ransacked and broken down, were well-nigh ruins

"The rooms appointit people to consider To hear God's Word where they should meet together, Are now convertit in sheep cots and faulds, Or else are fallen because nane them uphaulds; The Parish Kirk I ween they sae misguide, That nane for wind and rain therein may bide; Therefore, nae pleasure tak' they of the temple. Nor yet to come where nocht is to contemple. But craws and dows cryand and makand bare, That none thoroughly the minister may hear: But feathers, filth, and dung does lie abroad Where folk should sit to hear the Word of God."

This is a melancholy, still only true, description of the condition of the churches. According to the opinion of the General Assembly, the moral condition of the country in post-Eeformation times was awful, ugly heaps of all kinds of sin were lying in every corner of it, no part of it but what was overwhelmed with a spate. The old records of the period entirely bear out this statement. There was adamant want of organiza-tion. Nothing but chaos reigned." The Parliament which had established the Reformation in 1560 had never received the Royal sanction. It was not till 1581 that Presbyterianism as an ecclesiastical polity knew anything of systematised government. Then the Book of Constitutions Avas drawn up by the Reformed leaders, which, however, was not finally confirmed and established till 1592. The clergy appear to have had an exceptionally hard struggle. Most of them lived a beggar's life, for there was no provision made for stipends, owing to the avarice and selfishness of mean and unpatriotic nobles and lairds. Not many years after the Reformation the public-houses and alehouses were kept by the parish ministers, in order that they might eke out their miserable incomes. The matter was brought before the General Assembly in 1576, and it was laid down as a rule that " ane minister or reader that taps ale or beer or wine, and keeps an open tavern, should be exhorted to keep decorum," i. e. an orderly house. When matters began to show some signs of improvement, certain regulations came into operation throughout the parishes of Scotland. It was enacted in Parliament that each householder with 300 merks of yearly rent, and all substantial yeomen, should have a bible and a psalm-book, under a penalty of 10. It was decreed that each parish in the kingdom should advance 5 as a contribution 4: 13s. 4d. of this to go for payment of a copy to be " weel and sufficiently bund in paste and timmcr," and the remaining 6s. 8d. was to go for the expense of collecting the money. Anyone who dared to utter a word against the authority of the Holy Scriptures ran the risk of having his cars cropped and banished the parish. In 1580 there was an official appointed, whose duty it Avas to search every house in the realm and to require the sight of their bible and psalm-book, and to see that it was marked with their " ain name." Every house in the pari.-h had to be visited and every man had to produce his books, and npon every preaching day the parishioners had to shonlder their stools, called " creepies," and diligently attend divine service; otherwise they would have been branded as papists or heretics, and been severely punished. The introduction of the bible into Scottish homes wrought wonders. With much that was extravagant, gloomy, fanatical, and superstitious, there was mingled much reverence and sincere piety.

One of the most objectionable features of post-Eeformation times was the alarming extent to which professional begging prevailed. Doubtless this was occasioned by the multitudinous distractions of the age. When the country was rent and torn by civil and religious factions, its social condition was deplorable. In the Statute books of the period many regulations are to be found containing provisions for dealing with the hordes of vagabonds who Avandered at large over the land. Legislation seems, hoavever, to have entirely failed to check the evil. So far back as 1424 we find it enacted that "they that sal be thoiled to beg, sal have a certainne takinne (badge) on them," Avhile all those Avho had no tokens Avere to be " charged be open proclamation to labour and passe to craftis for Avinning of their living, under the pain of burning on the cheek and banishing of the countrie." Some years later it Avas enacted that "all stray beggars should have their ears nailed to the trone or till any other tree, and their eare cutted off, and they banished the country; and gif thereafter they be funden againe that they be hanged. Sornars that herrvis the King's lieges Avere to be put to death as thieves." By the Act of 1503 none Avere alloaved to beg except " cruiked folk, seik folk, impotent folk, and weak folk; and na beggars Avere thoiled to beir in ane parochin that were born in ane uther." These regulations having proved ineffectual, it was further enacted in 1579 that " all idle, strong beggars, loafers, and ruffians who would not work for their bread, should be weill scourged, and burnt through the eare with ane hot iron," thereafter to be hired out and compelled to work. Should this fail to reform them, they were to be hanged as thieves. Amongst the class recognised as subject to these penalties were " vagabone schollers of the Universities of St Andrewes, Glasgow, and Abirdene," not licensed by the University authorities to ask alms. Such stem regulations were passed for the most part in the interests of the really deserving poor, who were most difficult to maintain, owing to the frauds perpetrated upon the generously disposed by innumerable gangs of lazy, incorrigible vagabonds.

In 1590 the Kev. Alexander Tyrie was relieved of the charges of Tealing, Mains, and Strathmartine. In 1594 he was presented to the parsonage and vicarage of this parish by King James VI. In 1604 the Eev. David Kinneir became minister. By this time King James had gradually succeeded in undermining Presbyterian parity, previous to his attempt to enforce a system of Episcopal government, through the support he had obtained amongst the nobility and upper classes, many of whom accepted his dictum of " Xo Bishop, JSTo King." It is a very remarkable fact that throughout the long and bitter struggle which ensued between the Prelatists and Presbyterians the shire of Angus was keenly in favour of Prelacy; indeed, in this county centred the heart and soul of the Prelatic movement. The Synod of Angus was completely in unison with the Stewart policy, and was the first throughout the Church of Scotland to adopt that encroachment upon Presbyterian principle ventured upon by the King, viz., the appointment of constant Moderator, which was the thin end of the wedge for the introduction of a highdianded Episcopacy. In 1609 it was appointed that every preacher of God's Word hereafter shall wear black, grave, and comety apparel, beseeming men of their state and profession. On the 1st April 1610, 13 Bishops, 13 noble-men, 40 barons, and 100 ministers met for the establishment of Episcopacy, and Mr Kinneir was one of those who voted with the Prelatic party. He was again present at the Assembly of 1616, held in Aberdeen. At this time, therefore, the parish was under a full-blown Episcopal regime, and in charge of a keen Prelatic partisan. Xot the shadow of resistance was offered to such a complete overthrow of the fundamental principles of Presbyterianism by any one in the district, so far as we can discover. The people went like sheep with the nobility and clergy in favour of a Diocesan Episcopacy.

In 1630 a new church was built, which was the last specimen of early church architecture in Scotland. The plan of the church consisted of a chancel, 27 ft. by 21 ft. 5 in.; nave, 56 ft. 7 in. by 33 ft., Avith a square tower at west end. All the windows were square-topped, and of three lights, except the east one, which was of two lights, and placed in the gable. The chancel door was flat-headed. The nave was of semi-classic character, with a three-centred arched imposts and moulded jambs. On the north side both divisions of the church were blank. It was altogether a poor specimen of Scottish church architecture. Its only remarkable feature was one too characteristic of a poverty-stricken, uncultured, and inartistic age, viz.,

external and internal rudeness; altogether, a sad contrast to the beautiful Gothic structure, of former times.

A few relics of the old Romish churches still exist, the most

One of them, valuable and interesting of which are two fonts formed of the local grey sandstone, is a very early example, belonging, apparently, to the Norman transitional period, and, doubtless, contemporaneous with the ancient foundation. Like most of the Scottish fonts of its time, it has little to boast of in the way of ornamentation. Along its outer edge there is a slightly moulded depression, made possibly for the fitting in of the lead lining. The bowl is circular, and rests upon a diamond-shaped base, from which rise on two sides bands or supports, which are carried to the top. The chief feature of the font is the curious base. The dimensions are as follows:

Height of bowl, 7 inches. Diameter of orifice, 9 inches. Depth of orifice, 5 inches.

There is no drain. This font has all the appearance of having been built into the wall of the church. The other structure is a much larger font, and must have been principally used for baptismal purposes. It is of a massive character, and appears to have been originally embellished with decorative work, but this has been obliterated by mutilation and neglect. It belongs to the Norman period. The shape is octagonal, with a circular orifice. The upper portion, which contains the bowl, falls away in sharp lines to the centre, from which is carried out a broad and heavy base. The ornamentation consists of fillets and bold bead mouldings. In all probability this font was also used in Episcopal times. Its dimensions are as follows:

Height, 2 feet.

Diameter of orifice, 12 inches.
Depth of orifice, 9 inches.

There is a large bottom drain. The staple holes for the cover remain. There are also portions of the mullions of the large windows, and two quaint-looking dials. Underneath the session-house of the present church there is a very old burial vault, which, in all probability, was used in Romish times. It extended at one time the whole length of what, in olden times, was known as the Ramsay aisle; but it was subsequently reduced in size during alterations. It is of considerable size, and contains the mouldering remains of many representatives of the old Angus families of the Buchans, Ogilvies, and the Lyons of Strathmore. Not a monument, tablet, or inscription of any kind, however, has been permitted to remain within its walls.

The Rev. David Kinneir died in 1633, at the age of 52, after a ministry of 28 years. He was succeeded by the Rev. John Robertson, M. A., who had graduated at St Andrews in 1630. During his ministry the country generally was in a highly-troubled condition. The strife fomented over the service book was bitter in the extreme. The National League and Covenant had been drawn up, which was followed by the still more exciting and memorable days of the Solemn League and Covenant. In 1638 the first General Assembly seen in Scotland for twenty years met in Glasgow Cathedral. It was a great occasion. People flocked to it from all parts of the country, and so strong did feeling run that not a few went to it fully armed. The Rev. John Robertson Avas present, and voted with the Presbyterians. The high-handed Episcopalian policy summarily received its quietus, the obnoxious service book was condemned, the book of ordination, the court of high commission were denounced, and kirk-sessions, presbyteries, and provincial synods were once more restored.

On the 8th December 1641, the Eev. John Eobertson was translated to Dundee. It is recorded that the " Town Council of Dundee made choice of Mr John Eobertson to be ane of their ordinary ministers, and appointit to be payit to him as ane agreeit stipend the soum of ane thousand and two hundred marks, togidder with his house maill money" i. e., compensation for rent. He was appointed to the third charge. This appointment was an extremely fortunate one; for it is stated that the Council in ane voice awarded Mr Eobertson, after ten years of his ministry, a gratuity of 300 mcrks. He appears to have been a man of considerable ability and force of character. During the siege of Dundee by the army of the Commonwealth, under General Monk in 1651, Mr Eobertson performed signal services, and distinguished himself by his devotion and courage. After the capture of the town he received very harsh treatment from Monk. When he ventured to remonstrate with the English commander for his merciless severity, and the brutality of his soldiery to his parishioners of whom a great many, comprising women and children, were butchered Monk flew into an ungovernable rage, and told him if he dared to proceed further he would be compelled to scobe his mouth. For the zeal he had displayed, and his fearless and outspoken language, he and others were made prisoners, and despatched by sea to London, and there consigned to the Tower. All the prisoners suffered severely from their confinement. After a year's imprisonment they were released, and permitted to return to Scotland. Upon Mr Eobertson's return to Dundee, General Monk, who was still in command over the whole of Scotland, and Avho apparently seemed still to maintain hostile feelings towards him, ordered him to be consigned as prisoner to the Tolbooth of Dundee. After an imprisonment of several months, the Town Council petitioned Cromwell's Council for his release, which was ultimately granted.

In 1641 the Eev. William Wemyss became Minister of Aucliterhouse. Although the Church was everywhere supreme, still violent controversies soon arose between the two great rival factions-the Resolutioners and Protesters. The character of the times will be better understood from the entries which occur in the parochial records. In quoting these records we shall modernise the spelling in most cases, in order to render them the more intelligible, and venture upon some explanatory observations as we proceed on any points which bear upon former ecclesiastial life and authority.

May 25, 1645.-There was but ane preaching because of the enemy lying so near hand.

"When the Scottish people were convinced that King Charles I. was determined to force his high and mighty Episcopal government upon them, they accordingly resolved to resist his harsh and unreasonable encroachments upon their civil and religious liberties to the death. Those who had respect for their dearly-bought liberties combined and showed a bold front to the common enemy. Argyll came to the front as the chief political adviser, and Montrose was selected as the military leader of the Covenanters. The King reckoned himself superior to all opposition. The Marquis of Huntly was soon in the field with a Royalist force, which, however, was completely defeated and dispersed by the army of the Covenanters, through the superior military genius of Montrose. In Montrose the Covenanters had discovered one who was a tower of strength to their cause, and their success seemed certain.

The strife between the stubborn and ill-advised Monarch and the Covenanters daily grew more intense, and a protracted and sanguinary struggle seemed inevitable. The keen feeling and grim religious fanaticism manifested by the latter against those who had so recklessly trampled upon their rights and liberties, and sought to endanger the much-prized Reformed principles, had stirred up dangerous elements. In the manifesto issued by the Scots when they entered England under Lesly, in 1G40, it was boldly announced by those uncompromising soldiers, that they aimed at suppressing and punishing in a legal way those who are the troublers of Israel, the firebrands of hell, the Corahs, the Balaams, the Doegs, the Rabshakehs, the Hamansj the Tobiahs, and Sanballats of our time. Which done, we are satisfied. Scotland shall be reformed. Papists, Prelates, and all the members of the anti-Christian hierarchy shall pack from hence. The Lord shall be one, and His name one, throughout the whole island, which shall be glory to God, honour to the King, joy to the kingdom, comfort t) the posterity, example to other Christian kirks, and confusion to the incorrigible enemies. Words like these, backed up by a solid national party, and a strong and admirably-appointed army, did not fail to make a profound impression. When the Blue Bonnets marched over the border the enemy began to realise the powerful character of the opposition he had to confront, and the utter futility of the old tyrannical policy.

The King, for the first time, therefore, saw that he had blundered in his negotiations with the nobility, and at once en-deavourej. to accomplish by the wiles of diplomacy what he was unable to effect by force of arms. His secret negotiations with the ambitious Montrose ultimately proved successful, and in a short time the pet soldier-chief of the Covenanters disowned the Covenant, and raised the Royal standard. At this time the whole of Angus was thrown into excitement by his achievements, for he was credited with having no equal as a brilliant and accomplished strategist. With a strong but undisciplined body of Highlanders, drawn from the clans of the Gordons, the Macdonells of Glengarry, the Macphersons of Badenoch and Athole, and the clansmen of Clanranald, he had already defeated General Hurrie at Auldearn, and with characteristic alacrity and audacity descended upon Strathmore, with the intention of drawing into battle a force of Covenanters then holding the Castle of Xewtyle, under the Earl of Crawford. This nobleman, who had just assumed command, had severely ridiculed and condemned the military capacity of Argyll, whose colours had heen lowered in every encounter hitherto with his ahle antagonist, and was apparently exceedingly desirous of coming to close quarters with Montrose. The latter, however,, anticipated a victory over this neaV Preshyterian leader; hub intelligence having reached him that General Baillie was laying waste the country of the Clan Gordon, in the absence of its righting men, he hurriedly and unexpectedly abandoned the attack. It was, however, alleged that treachery had heen in operation, and that the Gordons really deserted. The expediency of having hut " ane preaching," in the circumstances, is pardonable. Those who were favourable to the Covenant were under arms. The parishioners had also heard of what had transpired in the previous month of April, when Montrose broke from the mountains, descended upon Dundee, and gave it up for plunder to his wild Highland and Irish levies. The town at this time was one of the wealthiest in Scotland, and had been lavish in its expenditure to suppress the rebellion of Moutrose.

June 8, 1645. The Beadle was appointed to summon Andrew Smith to begin his repentance.

The beadle of the Reformed Church was practically the successor of the Ostiarius of the Romish Church. The Ostiarius was the church officer and doorkeeper. He was ordained to his office, and was recognised as a member of the regular ecclesiastical staff. His instructions were to be most faithful in his attention to the house of God by day and night, to open the church doors to the faithful at certain hours, and keep them rigidly closed against the unfaithful. He had full authority to expel all heretics and excommunicated persons. He was also instructed to prevent all buying and selling within the building, to exclude beggars, to drive out dogs and other animals, to look after loiterers and sleepers, and maintain all clue order within the sacred edifice. In the Reformed Church the beadle or bedellus was also a civil officer acting under the kirk-session. One of his principal duties in times of stern discipline was to exercise citations. The beadle was also custodier of the jougs, branks, sackcloth, and other paraphernalia provided by kirk-sessions for the castigation of offenders. He was a prominent figure on the preaching days. He not unfrequently made the round of the church armed with a stick having a cleek on the end of it. When any woman was observed coming into the church with her plaid over her head or face, he at once applied his cleek to it, and the woman had either to put on her plaid correctly or leave it in the beadle's possession. If the same functionary noticed any outrageous head attire, he at once applied his cleek to the offending article and dragged it off. At stated intervals he had to go round the church to " wauken sleepers, to drive out the dogs, and remove greetin' bairns." When making these rounds he frequently carried a pot of tar and a brush, and the waukening was accomplished by a vigorous application of the tar brush to the sleeper's face. The tar brush was a weapon peculiarly efficacious, in the estimation of old Angus beadles, for the prevention and suppression of church sleeping.

The minister sent the beadle to warn certain people in the parish to prepare to oppose the enemy on the 5th July. Intimation was also made from the pulpit to those who were to assist on the 5th July.

The Rev. Mr Wemyss was apparently a man of considerable courage, and a sturdy upholder of the kirk militant. As a true Presbyterian, he made it a matter of duty to call upon the parishioners to obey the instructions sent down by the Presbyterian leaders. A general muster of all those capable of bearing arms was fixed to take place at Perth, then the headquarters of the Covenanting forces. Minister and beadle seem to have done what they could to rouse the farmers, shepherds, tradesmen, and servants of the parish to put on the blue bonnet, shoulder the pike, and join in the struggle with the Covenanters against Montrose. Men of every age, rank, and condition were now pressed into the Covenanters' ranks. All who resisted were c; subjected, to plentiful anathemas, and found it expedient to abscond. The farmers who possessed good strong horses were appointed to the cavalry, and the others to infantry regiments. It was an exceedingly raw, undisciplined, and somewhat grotesque force, and one by no means well adapted for the usages of Avar. It was no unusual practice for the minister of the parish also to set out fully armed and mounted with the others, and wield his sword with good effect in the encounters of these strangely fanatical times. Every company had a flag imprinted with the Scottish arms, and the Avords "For Christ's Crown and Covenant" stamped in golden letters.

Sunday, 20th July 1645. There AA as no preaching because of the enemy lying so near the town.

It is very evident that the movements of the Highland marauders had considerably upset the Sunday's proceedings, and that the parishioners had a most lively experience of the troubles of the civil Avar. The military tactics pursued by Montrose consisted of dexterous manoeuvring, rapid marches, and surprises. AVithoutthe slightest Avarning, he swept doavn upon his opponents, and on such occasions the helpless peasantry suffered severely. At this time Montrose had received intelligence of the concentration of the Covenanters at Perth, and Avas marching through Strathmore to attack them. In the course of the expedition the clansmen encamped at Auchtertyre Hill, Avhile bodies of Highlanders scoured the neighbourhood for cattle, sheep, and anything in the shape of plunder. What is still Avell-knoavn as Graham's Knoave, doubtless is the exact locality occupied by Montrose and his personal staff.

Thursday, April 30th, 1646. There Avas a fast-day, and that clay intimation Avas made that communion Avould be given on Sunday next, the preparation day being Saturday, at tavo o'clock. That day an Act was passed that Avhosoever came not to preparation sermon should pay 6 sh. Scots.

The fast-day here referred to Avas not Avhat is generally knoavn as the Sacramental fast. It Avas simply one of those days en- joined by the General Assembly to be observed on certain special occasions for religions fasting, humiliation, and self-mortification. It enjoined total abstinence, not only from food (unless bodily weakness so manifestly disable from holding out till the fast be ended, in which case somewhat may be taken, yet very sparingly, to support nature when ready to faint), but also from all worldly labours, discourses, and thoughts: from ail worldly delights, rich apparel, ornaments, gaudish attire, and vanities of either sex. Such an occasion as the fast-day in connection with the Communion was unknown till 1655, when it was introduced by the Protesters, who entirely changed the former methods of celebrating the Communion in Scotland. The only Act which. speaks of a special preparatory service on a week day is the Supplementary Act of 1645, which enjoins, before the celebration of the Communion, that there be one sermon of preparation delivered in the ordinary place of worship on that day immediately preceding. Even this innovation appears to have been unpopular, from the fact that it was necessary to impose fines in cases of non-attendance. On the same day Edward Montago, in Pitpointie, gave in his bill of complaint upon Janet Thomson, servant to Kobert Turnbull, in Cottoun, for slandering him behind his back. Slandering at this time was a serious offence. If any man or woman in a parish was found guilty of spreading evil stories about their neighbours, he or she might be compelled to stand up before the congregation and cry out " Tongue, ye lied; tongue, ye lied," for the first offence. For the second offence, a long seat on the cock stool or repentance stool was required. For the third offence, banishment from the parish. If any woman had become notorious for flyting and scolding, she was at once handed over to the tender mercies of the beadle, who fastened her up in the jougs, or put an iron hood, called the branks, over her head. The branks contained a formidable iron tongue, which was thrust well into the virago's mouth, and closed it up completely for some hours. Kesistance to such regulations was impossible. Whosoever presumed to disobey were excommunicated, had every door by order closed against them, were deprived of property, and were firmly believed to have passed into perdition.

May 3rd, 1646. Those appointed to attend collection at communion and serve tables are Mr Robert Hay of Dronlaw, John Wemyss, chamberlain to Earl of Buchan; William Christie of Balbeuchlie; James Watson, David Rodger, David Walker, David Thain, James Mann.

May 10th, 1646. The adulterer, John Mann, was enjoined by session to begin his repentance on Sunday next, in sackcloth.

Adulterers, according to the law of the church, were to be classed with malefactors. All persons convicted of such and similar offences might be thus punished. For the first fault, the man, as well as the woman, shall pay the sum of forty pound, otherwise both shall be imprisoned for the space of eight days, and be fed on bread and small drink, and afterwards shall be presented at the marketplace of the town or parish bareheaded, and there stand fastened for the space of two hours. For the second fault, they shall pay the sum of an hundred merks, otherwise the days of imprisonment shall be doubled, and their food shall be bread and water allenarly, and in the end they shall be presented at the market-place, and the heads of both shall be shaven. For the third fault they shall pay an hundred pounds, or else their imprisonment shall be tripled, and their food be bread and water allenarly, and in the end they shall be taken to the deepest and foulest pool or water of the town or parish and be there thrice douked, and afterwards banished the town or parish for ever. The pecunial fines which shall be received shall be keeped in a close box and converted ad pios usus in the parts where the crime was committed Acts 1567 and 1649-12. By the Act of 1661, the justices of the peace were empowered to put in execution the Acts of Parliament made for the punishment of persons convicted of such offences, and shall levy for the first fault, from a nobleman, four hundred pounds; from a baron, two hundred; from a gentlemen or burgess, one hundred; and from every other inferior person, ten pounds, Scots money, and these penalties shall be doubled according to the relapses and quality of the offenders. These penalties shall be levied not only from the man but from the woman according to her quality and degree of the offence, and shall be disposed off ad pios usus.

May 10th, 1646. A. B. (name illegible) was ordained to be put into the jougs.

The jougs were frequently called into requisition at this time. These were strong clasped iron collars fastened by means of a chain to the main entrance of the church. To be tied up by the neck in the jougs for several hours, to be compelled to submit to the shouts, jeers, and laughter of the village rabble, to be tortured by receiving on the head and face a wonderful variety of offensive articles from local urchins, not to speak of sundry kicks and blows, must have been an experience long to be remembered even by the most hardened offenders.

May 10th, 1646. David and Patrick Martins, in Balbeuehlie, in respect of their misbehaviour on Communion Sunday by drinking excessively, are ordained on the following Sunday to make their public repentance before the whole congregation, and pay their penalties.

All kirk-sessions were recommended to be vigorous, impartial, and yet prudent in the exercise of church discipline against all immorality especially drunkenness and filthiness, cursing and swearing, and profaning the Lord's Day. It was also recommended to ministers, Avhere the people sit too long in taverns, especially on the Saturday's night, through which some neglect the public worship of the Lord's Day, and others attend the worship drowsily, that they represent to the people, both publicly and privately, the sin and evil thereof, and call them to redeem that time which they have from business, and to employ it for converse with God about their soul's state, and in preparation for the Sabbath, which will yield more delight than all sensual pleasures will do.

Over-indulgence in strong ale within the alehouses before and after sermon was a common weakness in the country in olden times, and led to much trouble and heavy fining. Total abstinence was a virtue practically unknown. Moderation was strictly enjoined. None were to remain " langer in an aill house nor a pint aill or chapin aill the hand," but the caution, unfortunately, was useless. Threats of being " brankit, stockit, dookit, bainishit ye paroch," were all unavailing alongside of the temptations of the large and flowing ale-bicker.

Thursday, May 11th, 1646 John Petrie and Jean Walker, in Balbeuchlie, were married in the face of Christ's congregation.

All marriages were enjoined to be made in the face of the congregation after proclamation. According to the First Book of Discipline, marriage is not to be secretly used; but in open face and public audience of the kirk, and the Sunday before noon we think most expedient. Marriages, accordingly, were frequently celebrated on Sunday. Many scandals having arisen from this practice, the Avhole question was dealt with by the Assembly of 1645, and it was ordained that marriages should be solemnised on Thursdays, within the church, that day being the weekly lecture day. Occasionally marriages were celebrated on other days, but never for a very lengthened period, outside of the church. All private marriages were irregular. Clandestine marriages were severely proceeded against. The minister who officiated at such a marriage was ordered to be banished, and never to return on pain of death. Those who attempted any such irregularity were liable to heavy fines and imprisonment.

July 5th, 1646. The minister intimated from the pulpit that the Earl of Seaforth had been excommunicated.

To be excommunicated, excluded from the privileges of the church, and banished from the society of the faithful, meant simply ruin and social death. Excommunicated persons who entered the congregation during the ministration of the Sacraments or common prayers were to he apprehended and delivered to the Judge Ordinary, who shall keep them in prison till they find caution under such sums as the minister shall modify (1585, James VI.) jsTo persons who are or shall he excommunicated are allowed directly or indirectly to enjoy the possession of their lands, rents, and revenues; hut the same shall he intromitted with and uplifted for His Majesty's use (James VI., 1609). These Acts remained in force till 1690, when civil pains for such sentenceswere rescinded; and in Queenanne's reign it was ordained that no civil pain or forfeiture or disability whatever should he incurred by any person by reason of any excommunication or prosecution by the Church judicators in Scotland. This sentence was passed by the Presbyterians upon Seaforth because he was understood to be a renegade.

After the battle of Inverloclry, Montrose marched to Elgin. Thence he penetrated into Moray, after issuing a proclamation, in which he commanded all the men of the province between sixteen and sixty years of age to join his ranks, or take the consecaiences of refusal. Overawed by those threats and penalties, the Earl of Seaforth, chief of the Mackenzies who was in command of the northern Covenanters the Grant, and other chiefs renounced the Covenant. For this breach of allegiance Seaforth was accordingly excommunicated by the Covenanting party. As soon, however, as he escaped out of the hands of Montrose he very wisely rejoined the Covenanting army.

July 9th, 1646. A fast was keepit, and twice preaching.

Fasts, or special days of humiliation, were frequently held during the exciting days of the Covenant and the Civil War. They consisted for the most part of special religious services for the grievous sins and provocations of the land. The most important were associated with some special national emergency. Many, however, were held in times of storms, fires, threatened famines, droughts, floods, plagues, unusual visitations of distress, remarkable celestial phenomena in short, anything which particularly impressed the superstitious minds of the age, called for self-examination and humiliation. Certain grave calamities, believed to have been occasioned by witches, charmers, sorcerers, and other agents of the evil one, also called for humiliation. It must be admitted that not a few fasts were held for reasons which in an age of intelligence would be reckoned quite absurd. On the occasion of the fast referred to in the entry there was twice preaching; but this was a very short service compared with many of the period. Burnett tells us that on one fast-day, in a certain parish, there were six sermons preached without intermission " I was there myself, and not a little weary of so tedious a service."

July 18th, 1646. Jean Morris was on the stool of repentance for the sixth time, and was absolvit.

August 2nd, 1646. Agnes Croile, in Dronlaw, was three several times on stool of repentance, and absolvit.

As the jougs and branks had superseded the old " nailing up by the lug" practice, so gradually the "stool" comes into greater prominence throughout these records. This important article of kirk-session furniture of the past still exists, and notwithstanding its age and vicissitudes is wonderfully sound. It is a substantial four-legged article, made of the best of oak, and from its dimensions could easily have accommodated two offenders if placed back to back. The rej)entance stool was, as a ride, ostentatiously placed by its faithful guardian, the beadle, immediately in front of the pulpit, and upon it the offender had patiently to sit out the required appearances, and listen, moreover, to a severe castigation from the pulpit.

August 28th, 1646. On that day a collection was made for distressed people of Cullen, who had their town burnt.

This was one of the northern towns which opposed "Montrose on his victorious march through the Northern Counties. For such opposition it was ruthlessly consigned to the flames, and its inhabitants rendered destitute.

September 4th, 1646. David, in Scotston, gave in his hill of complaint against John Gullan, his tenant, for slandering him in saying that he took two of his sheep and slew them in his own house, and gave them to him while working to him.

September 27th, 1646. The minister intimated a fast for next Sabbath; likewise he read out of pulpit the names of those who were excommunicated by Mr Robert Blair, Kirk of Edinburgh, to wit, the Earl of Airlie, Sir Alexander M'Donald, and some others.

By the Parliament of 1645, Lord Airlie and his sons-Sir Thomas Ogilvy and Sir David Ogilvy along with other supporters of Montrose, were found "gilty of heigh tressone, and forfaultes ther lyffes, honours, tytles, landes. and glides, and decerns the same to belong to the publicke for defraying the oharge of the warr, as lykwayes the saides estaites in one woyce ordaines the Lyone King of Armes to delait their armes out of lies registers and bookes of honor, to rent the same wut all convenit solemity in the Parliament Housse, and at the Crosse of Edinburghe publickly."

The name of Alexander Macdonald was one of the best known in Scotland at this time. He was proud of being the uncompromising foe of Argyll, and ever a stout upholder of the Royalist cause in the Western Highlands. By his countrymen he was known as Alastair Maccolla, and in the historical records he appears under the names of Colkitto, young Colkitto, Colonel Kitteach, c. He was a man of considerable ability; but was chiefly remarkable for his great physical strength and ferocity on the battlefield. He had the reputation among the clans of being the strongest man in Scotland. When an officer was about to be selected to take command of the division of Irish soldiers which had been raised in Antrim for Montrose, it was decided that the command should be bestowed upon the man who possessed the strongest arms. Colkitto, baring his arms, astonished all by their formidable muscular proportions. His physical superiority being undisputed, he became the chief of the Irish levies. He was present at the battle of Inverlochy, and was credited with having slain twenty men with his own hand. He carried his depredations to such an extent throughout the county of Argyle that he used to boast that the crow of a cock could not be heard nor the smoke of a chimney seen within twenty miles of Inveraray. Throughout the Civil War he was recognised as one of the best officers of Montrose. He Avas devoted to the Marquis, simply because he was the rival of his great enemy. He was present at the sacking of Dundee, and it was he who plundered and burned Coupar Angus by the orders of Montrose. This turbulent and dangerous character in many ways left traces of his vengeance throughout Angus. When Colkitto was upon a marauding expedition with his semi-savage Irish followers, he was the terror of all, because his operations were conducted with the greatest cruelty and unnecessary severity. When any prominent antagonist fell into his hands, he gave him the choice of heading or hanging. Colkitto was subsequently slain in an engagement in Ireland, after a very remarkable career, for the most part spent in sanguinary private feuds and ceaseless warfare.

September 27th, 164(3. Isabel Gall, in Leoch, did complain to session upon Janet Thomson, servant to Robert Turnbull, for slandering her and calling her a witch and thief, and the kirk-officer was ordained to warn her to session 4th October. At the same time several notorious flyters and scolders were sharply dealt with.

October 18th, 1646. The slanderer, John Gulland, was ordained for his slander to appear three several Sabbaths on stool of repentance in sackcloth. On this day John Moram appeared on stool and in sackcloth for the twenty-fifth time.

The number of appearances required for breaches of the Seventh

Commandment was twenty-five, and throughout in sackcloth. On such occasions the culprit was compelled to exchange the usual Sunday best for a shabby old cloak made of sackcloth or old linen. The character of the garment by no means improved the appearance of the offender. His situation provoked many a groan from the stern administrators of discipline, and a satisfactory smile from those who had previously occupied the same position.

September 16th, 1647. Andrew Doig, in Scotston, was before the session for shearing on the Sabbath day, and whs ordained to make his public repentance and to pay 20 sh.

By the Act of 1579, it was ordained that 'ma handie-labouring nor working be used on the Sabbath day, nor na gamming and playing, passing to tavernes and aile-houses, or selling of meat or drink, or wilful remaining from their paroche kirk," under pain of fines. Failing payment, the offender was to be put in the stocks or sik other engine. By the Act of 1594, it was ordained that " quha-sum-ever prophains the Sabbath day by selling or offering for sale ony gudes, gear, or quhat-sum-ever merchandise themselves, or by another, for a third offence their haile gudes and gear shall be eschetted to the King."

Sabbath observance was therefore most strictly enjoined. No one was allowed to go from one place to another on Sunday, no matter what the business might be. No one was allowed to visit a friend. No stranger was permitted to reside in a parish unless he went to the preachings. Every husband was answerable for his wife's behaviour, and every master for his servants. Every man was bound to be in church at both diets of worship. Ministers would not listen to the modern excuses for non-attendance, such as " splittin' pains in the head and back, fell attacks of rheums, tarrible coughs, bad roads, and weet, blawy Sundays." Such excuses would not for a moment have been accepted or tolerated. If an elder or deacon was absent from the preaching, that meant a fine of 2 sh.; others, again, were fined 6d. Church attendance and all due decorum within the church were also rigidly enforced. Xo women were allowed to get away into the corners of the church or behind pillars, for it was observed that they were too often in the habit of wrapping their plaids round their heads and falling sound asleep during the preaching. Those troubled with this weakness were requested to bring their stools and sit down right in front of the minister, and under the beadle's vigilant eye. An old poem of the times exhibits this feminine weakness:

"But as for ine,
Sic unca sights I never see,
For soon as oot the text I read,
I draw my rogullay roond my heid,
An' fast asleep I soon fa' ower
It's better than through the kirk to glower."

Sept. 19th, 1647. John Gulland and Janet Lyall to be summoned to declare whether they heard William Robertson say that Thomas Reid took his lint out of the burn.

On that day there was a thanksgiving made for victory over the common enemy. This Avas the victory obtained by General David Leslie over the forces of the Marquis of Huntly, who had continued to hold out for the Cavaliers. The Marquis had fallen back before a powerful body of Covenanters upon the mountainous district of Eadenoch, into which he was boldly followed and defeated. Other victories followed over smaller detachments in the Western Highlands. Several of the chief officers were made prisoners, and afterwards executed. The Marquis himself was shortly afterwards captured in Strathdon, imprisoned, and finally executed. This important victory was celebrated by a general thanksgiving throughout the country.

On the same day, Mr Robert Hay of Dronlaw and Mr James Wemyss were ordained to gather church collection for distressed people of Brechin.

This town was for some time the headquarters of the Covenanting army under the Marquis of Argyll, and in its vicinity many skirmishes took place with Montrose's troops. Some time afterwards it was taken by Montrose, who ordered it to be burned to the ground. In 1647, Brechin also suffered severely from the ravages of the plague. Within a few months about 600 of the inhabitants became the victims of this terrible scourge.

At a meeting of the Scottish Parliament, held on 23rd Dec. 1645, a petition was presented by the toune of Brechin to the estates showing " that ther towne lies beine twa several times plundered and vasted by the enimey, and desyres that they may be exeimepted from payment of ther twa monthes maintenance and have repartitione of ther grate losses for ther present subsistence."

Sunday, 11th October 1647. Thomas Euthven was before session for striking of his wife and causing her to blood. It was ordained that he come next dnj and make his repentance before the session, and thereafter that he and his wife be brought before session and reconciled, and Avarned if the like break out again the instigators would be punished.

November 7th, 1647. Owing to emptiness of box, and as there are some supplicants recommended by General Assembly to the Presbytery, it was ordained to gather collection for their supply.

The only collections taken by order of the General Assembly were for the poor. The poverty which existed throughout the country to a large extent occasioned by the troubles of the Civil War was very great; consequently, requests for collections for deserving poor were frequent. Upon the church fell the burden of maintenance. To prevent imposition by " Strang" beggars and vagabonds, who were too plentiful, it was customary for kirk-sessions to grant licenses to the really deserving poor and distressed permitting them to beg, and leaden badges were given to them to be worn round their neck to distinguish them from the lazy, worthless, and incorrigible. Only beggars thus specially licensed were permitted to congregate at church doors,.

or on such occasions as marriages, baptisms, and funerals. The church was their chief rendezvous. At every service some were present, and directed the attention of those who entered the church to their poverty by pulling at their coats and dresses.

January 9th, 1648. ELspeth Webster, the adulteress, being twenty-five several Sabbaths in sackcloth, was absolvit.

January 27th, 1648. There was an Act passed by session that whatever man or woman was found in fornication after this each of them should pay 4.

Scots currency was only 1-12th the value of sterling. 1 Scots = Is. 8d. sterling. The suppression of immorality was attempted by many Acts, but they all seem to have failed to produce a satisfactory standard of public morality. The branks, jougs, stool, sackcloth, c, seem to have been by no means effective deterrents. The system of heavy fining was accordingly introduced. Such fines, besides acting as restraints from vice, were doubtless imposed also with the view of helping the parochial finances, which appear to have been in an unsatisfactory condition, and quite unequal to the demands made upon the " box."

January 30th, 1648. William Gray, of the Kirktoun, by the consent of " yee sessione was nominat for to be yee beadle," and promised to be honest and faithful in his calling, and was ordained to receive for every grave he made 10 sh.

By the Act of 1576 all burials were prohibited from being-made in the church. All contraveners of the Act were ordered to be suspended from church privileges. It had been previously ordained that a bier should be made in every country parish to carry the dead to the burial place, and that those of the villages or houses adjacent should convey the body to the burial place, and bury it six feet under the earth.

May 7th, 1648. Walter Thomson and James Watson were ordained to search the alehouses during sermon.

The elders of this period were practically parochial police. By the law of the Church, each elder had a special district assigned to him, and was held responsible for the maintenance within it of good order. Visitation of their districts at least once a month was strictly enjoined. All alehouses were placed under their immediate supervision. The keepers of these houses were strictly enjoined, under heavy penalties, to keep proper hours and maintain good order. They were permitted, as a ride, to keep open till ten o'clock; if not closed, however, by that time, a visitation was made, and the house cleared at once by the elders. This was the origin of the well-known saying that ten o'clock is elders' hours. "When any individuals were missed from church, the elders hurried out, and were on the search at once. If the absentees were not found within their homes, then a search of the alehouses ensued. If any persons were discovered, their names were at once taken down, reports given in, citations issued, and the usual penalties quickly followed.

May 21st, 1648. That day it was concluded by the minister and session that there, should be ane school built.

Prior to the Eeformation the monasteries were centres of learning, and the monks the only teachers. In most of the religious houses education was imparted, but only to members of the great baronial families and freeholders. In the reign of King James IV. the nobles were compelled to have their sons educated, under heavy penalties. In the Eeformed Church the Look of Policy recommended that there should be a schoolmaster able to teach grammar and the Latin tongue where there is a town of any reputation, and in landward parishes that the reader or minister take charge of the youth of the parish to instruct them in the rudiments, particularly in the Catechism of Geneva. It was also enjoined that youths be " brocht up and instructed in the fear of God and gude manners." Learning the Lord's Prayer, the Commandments, " belev" and heads of the Catechism demanded for examination before communion, were specially mentioned. Tor many years the education of the young in country parishes was conducted by the parish minister, who was the only man competent for the task. The clergy did their utmost to advance education, hut the poverty of the country militated sadly against its advancement. There was no legal obligation for the parishioners maintaining a school. By the Acts of Parliament, 1633 and 1646, it was recommended to the several Presbyteries to see to the settling of schools in every landward parish, where children were to he taught reading, writing, and the grounds of religion. Previous-to 1646, the majority of landward parishes had no schools.

By the Act of 1646 a commodious house was to be provided for the school, and the schoolmaster's salary was ordained not to be under one hundred merks, nor above two hundred merks. equal to.-) lis. 1M. and 11 2s. 2 d. sterling. The heritors Avere not obliged to provide a house of greater accommodation than two rooms, including kitchen. A garden of at least part of an acre was also allowed. It was optional to assign, in lieu of such garden, an addition to his salary at the rate of eight bolls of oatmeal per acre. From a subsequent entry it appears-the schoolhouse was not erected for some time. There were, however, certain small sums expended upon repairing the " Maister's Chaumber."

July 1648. Intimation was made from the pulpit about distribution of money to those killed or hurt in the Duke's-engagement in England.

When King Charles I. Avas a prisoner at Carisbrook Castle, in the Isle of Wight, during 1647, the Earls of Lanark and Lauderdale succeeded in obtaining a private intervieaV Avith him. At this interview a secret treaty Avas formed, by winch those nobles engaged to raise an army in Scotland in the interests of the King to enable him to regain his liberty and throne, Avhilst the King, on his part, engaged conditionally to confirm Presby-terianism. On three different occasions Scotland had mustered an army, and sent it forth in defence of the National Covenant; now Ave find the same army going forth under the Duke of Hamilton in favour of the King against the Republican army under Cromwell. In the Parliament of lltli March 1648, the Royalists, being in a majority, succeeded in carrying a vote which provided for an army 40,000 strong. Great opposition was made to this Engagement by the leaders of the Church, and a proclamation against it was issued. In the opinion of Argyll's supporters, it was " nothing but a snare to lead souls to damnation." The ablest of the Scottish generals, the Earl of Leven and David Leslie, refused commands. The opposition produced so much effect upon the popular mind that the force levied fell very considerably below what was anticipated. With an army of 15,000 men, hastily levied, undisciplined, and badly equipped, Hamilton crossed the English border. Considerably reinforced by a body of English loyalists he continued his march. Henceforward, however, nothing but misfortune attended the expedition. The whole military operations were conducted with such utter incapacity and cowardice that disaster was inevitable. Hamilton ordered Munro, an officer of considerable experience, to remain in Westmoreland with a strong division, while he advanced. Although he had entered Lancashire, and was now in touch with highly-disciplined troops led by Cromwell himself, his army was still broken up and distributed over a considerable area. When the Scots were thus so wretchedly commanded, entirely disorganised, and unprepared to resist the slightest opposition, Cromwell with his cavalry thundered suddenly down upon Hamilton's division, and drove it back in precipitate disorder upon Preston. Instead of Hamilton holding the town, and endeavouring to rally his troops and maintain his position till the rest of his troops concentrated from the neighbourhood, nothing short of an ignominious retreat followed. The infantry thus ignobly abandoned and unsupported, threw down their arms, implored for quarter, and unconditionally surrendered to the victorious Ironsides. Hamilton with his cavalry having escaped from Preston, lapsed once more into such a state of helplessness and inactivity that he was overtaken by Colonel Lambert, completely surrounded, and finally forced to capitulate.

Hamilton was thrown into prison. Many of the officers succeeded in effecting their escape by bribery, but the common soldiers suffered great hardships at the hands of the victors. Never did such failure and disaster accompany the Scottish arms as they did throughout the engagement. The execution of the King followed in 1649, and shortly afterwards Hamilton met the same fate. The despatch of the Scottish army into England led to the invasion of Scotland by Cromwell and innumerable troubles, of which the town of Dundee had an ever-memorable experience.

August 5th, 1648. On that day there were four score and sixteen pounds which came from the army, given to soldiers who were lamed and who were killed in my Lord Dudhope his regiment.

Lord Dudhope previously known as the Laird of Dudhope was a strong Royalist partisan, and had succeeded in raising a regiment of troopers from the county, which subsequently shared in the reverses of the Engagement. This quaint intimation of the distribution of military funds implies that a number of engagers had been raised from the parish, through the influence of the Earl of Buchan. When the defeated engagers reached Westmoreland they were joined by the force which had been left there under General Munro. With all possible haste they proceeded to Scotland. Not far from the border they were met by the army of reserve, under the Earl of Lanark, brother of the unfortunate Hamilton. This nobleman, notwithstanding many grave doubts as to his military capacity, practically constituted himself at a council of war leader of the newly-raised army. It had been levied mainly by the efforts of the nobility and landed gentry, prominent among whom as one of the Earls Marischal of Scotland was the Earl of Buchan. It had the reputation of being a formidable and gallant army, and reckoned to be equally capable of defeating the opposition of Argyll, and resisting any invasion of the country by Cromwell. Such brilliant anticipations, however, were somewhat prematurely entertained, because very soon afterwards the Earl of Lanark, to the dismay and disgust of the Cavalier element, made a truce with Argyll, which practically constituted the latter master of the situation in Scotland. The next important event was Cromwell's invasion, conquest, and occupation of the country.

Octoher 1648. Two persons were brought to repentance for shearing corn on the Sabbath day.

November 29th, 1648. James Mann was ordained to go to John Monteith to get 40 sh. my Lord Buehan had promised to give for the upbringing of a Highland boy at the schools.

In 1648 every congregation throughout the Church was appointed to pay forty shillings Scots yearly for maintaining Highland boys, i. e., Gaelic-speaking boys, at school. Others were recommended to bursaries in Universities. A special effort was made at this time to spread education and the knowledge of religion throughout the Highlands and Islands, which appear to have made but slow advances in civilisation through neglect, poverty, and ignorance.

January 7th, 1649. The minister and two of the elders went through the church after sermon desiring the people to subscribe the Covenant.

On several important occasions covenants or bonds of union, by which the Scottish people bound themselves by solemn compacts in opposition to governments hostile to their religious principles, were drawn up. During the minority of King James (1581), a covenant was entered upon to protect the Reformed Church against the Catholics. This was renewed in 1588, when the country was threatened by the Spanish Armada. These two covenants, it will be observed, were directed solely against Popery. What was known again as the National Covenant of 1638, not only renounced the doctrines of Rome, but distinctly repudiated and condemned all Episcopal authority and pretension. It was also a compact to defend, against every assault, the discipline and doctrine of the Presbyterian Church. The Solemn League and Covenant referred to in the entry was the celebrated bond of union between the people of England and Scotland. It was adopted by the Parliament of 25th September 1643, and was directed mainly against Episcopal government. It consisted of six articles: 1. The preservation of the Reformed Church in Scotland, and the reformation of religion in England and Ireland. 2. The extirpation of Popery, Prelacy, Schism, c. 3. The preservation of the liberties of Parliament and the King's person and authority. 4. The discovery and punishment of all malignants, c. 5. The preservation of a blessed peace between these Kingdoms.

6. The assisting all who enter into the Covenant. This will Ave do as in the sight of God.

In this parish the people appear to have been very slow in giving their acceptance to this document, while others treated it with hostility and contempt. By the orders of the General Assembly a Parochial Committee was ordered to be formed in every parish, and that Committee had to see that each adult member of the parish signed, or otherwise gave his adhesion to, the Covenant. Heavy penalties were ordered to be enforced against all who were obstinate or slothful. At this time many of the parishioners were tainted with malignancy, and stubbornly opposed to dictation from Presbyterian headquarters.

March 10th, 1649. The kirk officer was ordained to go through the yairds of the Kirktown to see if there were any clothes drying, that they may be deferred to the kirk-session.

March 11th, 1649. Marjory Young and Janet Gowans were cited before session for contesting and striving together in church for seat.

This is a frequent entry in the records of this period. In former times the area of the church was left open, and people brought their stools with them, which not unfrequently were used as handy weapons, in the event of personal disputes arising within or without the church. In those days a preacher of erroneous doctrine ran great risk also of having one hurled at his head. The churches at this time were not, as a rule, fully supplied with fixed pews or " daskes" for the parishioners. Such were looked upon as luxuries, and were put up by the principal heritors for their own special use. Through the kindness of proprietors one or two were erected for their tenants; but these were by no means sufficient for the accommodation of all. Accordingly, the question resolved itself into that of first come first served. Free fights over the pews were very frequent, and certain female members of the congregation were not slow in applying physical force to such as ventured to deprive them of their highly-valued places in the " daskes." Long after the pew system was introduced, however, a church fight was by no means a rare occurrence in this parish.

March 24th, 1649. The kirk officer was ordained to summon Thomas Wylie to come and make his public repentance for threshing corn on the Sabbath day.

April 7th, 1649. There was an examination after second sermon.

In this year it was enacted that every minister, with the assistance of the elders, take course that in every house where there is any that can read, there be at least one copy of the Shorter and Larger Catechisms, Confession of Faith, and Directory for Family Worship, for a weekly catechising to be constantly observed in every kirk. Every Presbytery was also ordained to take trial of all the ministers within their bounds once at least in the half year, whether they be careful to keep weekly diets of catechising, and if they shall find any of their number negligent therein, that they be admonished for the first fault; and if after such admonition they do not amend, the Presbytery for the second fault shall rebuke them sharply, and if after such rebuke they do not amend, they shall be suspended.

The public examination and catechizing of parishioners as to their knowledge of the Scriptures Was therefore general throughout the seventeenth century. The inhabitants of a particular district within a parish were summoned to appear on a specified day and hour, and all were bound to attend. The roll was carefully called, and absentees were carefully marked, fined, and afterwards compelled to present themselves. There was no respect of persons shown.

May 1st, 1649. On that clay those who had not sworn to or subscribed the Covenant did both swear and suhscribe the same.

When the Scottish Parliament met on the 4th January 1649, one of its first duties was to deal with the insubordinate and turbulent. On that day the Marquis of Argyll made a very long speech, consisting of five heads, which he called the " brecking of the malignants' teith," at the same time informing the House that he quho was to speak after him (Warreston) " wold hrecke ther jawes." The Engagers had clearly broken their vows, and it was declared by an Act of Parliament that all individuals who had taken part in the "Engagement" were to he held as infamous, and incapable of ever again serving the State. The terms of this Act were clearly applicable to not a few within the parish, so that such persons had to make up their minds at once either to comply with the Act or suffer accordingly.

In September 1649, the province of Angus and Mearns was visited by a Committee of ministers and ruling elders for its " lowse lines." This Committee deprived eighteen ministers, and two expectants they silenced, five ministers they suspended, and two kirkis which had old failed men they ordained to be prowydit of new ministers.

May 12th, 1649. The elders were ordained to mak' search for any that did spread muck on Sunday after sermon.

October 28th, 1649. The minister did forewarn James, Earl of Buchan; George Sommer, Patrick Finrard, servitors to said Earl; and Thomas Gellies, servant to Thomas Mann, Burnhead, to go to Dundee to Presbytery, Wednesday, 31st October, to obey what the Presbytery had to object against them in going to the Engagement.

By the Act of 1646, it was appointed that such as after trial shall be found to have been in actual rebellion, and to have carried charge with the rebels, to have accepted commissions for raisin ' horse or foot to them, or have otherwise assisted them in manner mentioned in the Act, shall humbly acknowledge their offence upon their knees, first before the Presbytery, and thereafter before the congregation upon a Sabbath in some place before the pulpit. This is the explanation of Mr Wemyss' action against the parochial maiignants. He would give no quarter, and the offenders accordingly had to accompany him to the Presbytery of Dundee, and there give an account of themselves. It must have been a somewhat ludicrous spectacle to behold the three gallant troopers with their noble captain on their knees before the Presbytery, ignominiously surrendering to the upholders of the Solemn League and Covenant.

December 10th, 1G49. There were sundry Acts of Parliament concerning the Covenant, with the Covenant itself, read out of the pulpit, and intimation was made of a fast to be kept on Thursday, the 14th December.

Sunday, December 17th, 1640. The Covenant being read to the people, they all did swear to it. On that day Harry Kicky, servitor to the Karl of Buchan, confessed to the minister and elders that it was sore against their wills that they came in the night and took the people out of their beds to go into England.

The Engagers from this parish appear to have made their departure by moonlight. This surrender of the troopers to the minister and kirk-session shows that the party of Argyll was supreme, civilly and ecclesiastically, even in the most remote districts.

January 6th, 1650. The minister desired the session to make search everywhere in their own quarters if they knew of any witches or charmers in the parish, and delate them to the next session.

One of the most remarkable features of the time was the belief in witchcraft. Many persons, especially women, were supposed to have joined themselves to Satan. They were believed to sail through the air, to meet at midnight within the churches, to raise dreadful stoims, and to bring in all manner of diseases. Charges of the most extraordinary character were made against old women, and, as a rule, entirely believed. About 4,000 persons are believed to have perished through burning, strangling, and other horrible means. The victims were the aged, the weak, the deformed, the lame, the blind, the insane those poor creatures whom infirmities, years, and neglect had rendered wretched, and their judges and executioners were reckoned the most intelligent men of their day. Throughout Angus there was a general search for witches at this time, and several individuals suffered from the strange and horrible fanaticism. Several poor women Avere tortured and put to death in the county amid scenes of the most savage and revolting character. People flocked from all quarters to witness their fellow-creatures consigned to the flames, amid the jeers and laughter of an ignorant and superstitiously-blinded rabble. Ministers and elders even found it expedient in several instances to postpone church services in order that they and their fellow Christians might be present at such shocking displays of inhumanity. Here is the account rendered to a kirk-session in Fife for the burning of two witches. Tt speaks for itself, and affords striking evidence of the gross ignorance and fanaticism of the age. To Mr John Miller, when he went for a man to try them i. e., for a witch pricker, who pretended he could discover whether they were bona-fide witches or not by inserting long pins into their bodies 2 7s.; in purchasing the commission, 9 3s.; for ton loads of coal to burn them, 3 6s. 8d.; for a tar barrel, 14 s.; for towes, 6s.; to him that brought the executioner, 2 18s.; to the executioner for his pains, 8 14s.; for his expenses, 16s. 4d.

January 7th, 1650. James Euthven, John Black, Thomas Hill, and James Low were before the session for threshing corn on the fast-day. They were sharply reproved, and forbidden to do the like again. On that day the minister delivered to session the annual rent of 400 merks for use of schoolmaster and poor? which were given by Mary Douglas, elder of Drum.

The lady here referred to was well known for her unstinted generosity. It was she who received Lady Ogilvie into her house after she was driven from her residence of Forthour Castle, which was plundered before her eyes, and subsequently consigned to the flames by Inverawe, acting under the instructions of Argyll. Although homeless and destitute, all were forbidden to shelter or befriend her. The Lady of Drum wrote to Argyll asking permission to receive her grandchild, but he refused his consent. In defiance of his order she courageously received her, and befriended her in her house of Kelly.

February 10th, 1650. The minister warned people out of pulpit of an Act of General Assembly forbidding promiscuous dancing, and whosoever should henceforth be found doing contrary to said Act should be censured; also he warned people of Newton to come to be examined.

Presbyteries were ordered to take special care to restrain the abuses which took place at penny bridals, and also to censure the observers of lykewakes, and to use all possible means to suppress promiscuous dancing, and to censure all such as were found guilty of it.

The stern ultra-Presbyterians would tolerate no amusements. These were in their eyes wiles of the devil and the destroyers of souls. The grim cast-iron theology and wofully gloomy fanaticism so widely prevalent never for a moment could tolerate innocent recreation, nor come to accept the dictum that there is a time to dance. The entire social life of those days was weighed down by a harsh, superstitious, intolerant, ecclesiastical system. The tender, merciful, attractive side of Christianity was practically unknown. The charity that never faileth found few adherents. Pharisaism, violent bigotry, ecclesiastical partisanships flourished in full vigour, while the Christianity of Christ w T as practically supplanted by a spurious Calvinism.

February 24th, 1650. The people of the place were warned for catechizing. The people were appointed to come at ten o'clock, and Bonniton at two o'clock.

March 3rd, 1650. James Hayok, in Adamstone, was before-session for selling of a plaid on Sabbath day; but he showed that he sold the plaid on Wednesday before, and was cleared.

Form of testimonial of marriage from Mr Alexander Bruce,. Minister of Tealing, to Minister of Auchterhouse

Reverend, and Loving Brother, These are to inform you that James Fyffe, of Drum, Parish of Longforgan, and Christian Wintoun, in this parish, are proclaimed on three several Sabbath days in our church, and no impediment in the contrar, therefore they desire to be married in your church of Auchterhouse. Ye shall grant them the benefit whensoever ye shall be required thereto, provided always that he bring with him in testimonial from minister of Longforgan that they are proclaimed likewise there and nothing objected. Recommending you and all yours-to the Lord's blessing, I remain, your loving Brother,

Mr Alexander Bruce.

Testimonial from Mr Alexander Milne, of Longforgan

To all and sundry whom it effeirs, to whose knowledge thir presents come, we, minister and elders of Longforgan parish, wishing all health and happiness through Jesus Christ, do testify and declare by thir presents that the bearer, James Fyffe, of Dion, within the said parish, and Christian Wintoun, within the parish of Tealing, were, at the minister of Tealmg's request, lawfully proclaimed in a purpose of marriage at our church three several Sabbath days, according to the order of the church, without any impediment or objection, so that if it be thus in Tealing, we know nothing that may hinder the solemnisation of their marriage at the parties' desire in time convenient, as pleaseth God to direct, whilk to be of verity we testify of thir presents. Written by John Elder, Notar Scribe to our Session. Subscribed with our hands-as follows, at Longforgan, 10 March.

Signed by Minister for Session.

The granting of testimonials was general throughout the Church. In all cases of scandal such testimonials were refused. The preliminaries to marriage were conducted with great gravity, dignity, and formality. The character of the individuals was carefully sifted, and examination upon Bible knowledge was in many instances demanded, also certificates showing that the parties were diligent attenders upon Divine ordinances, besides those relating to due proclamation, had to be produced. The tabling of consignation fees was also strictly required.

April 7th, 1650. On that day there was a fast kept, tlie-causes thereof as follows:

Rev. Brother, The King's Majesty (King Charles I.), who lately-reigned, being now, contrary to the dissent and protestation of the kingdom, removed by a violent death, the estates of Parliament having declared and proclaimed the Prince of Scotland and of Wales to be King, as yon may perceive by the enclosed proclamation, and have resolved to make addresses to him with all possible speed about the things that concern the security of religion, and of the peace of the kingdom, and because of the great importance of His Majesty's deposition, and of these affairs, we hope you shall be careful to deal earnestly with God, both in private and in public, in behalf of His Majesty who now is; and we have now thought fit that a solemn public humiliation be kept on Thursday, the 22nd of this instant, as for all the sins and provocations of the land, so to pray the Lord, in a special manner, for these things following: 1. That he would deliver the King from evil counsel in which he is now involved, and teach him in his yoiith the knowledge of his way, that he may fear his name for establishing and advancing the kingdom of Jesus Christ, and the work of Reformation.

2. That the Lord will be pleased to bless these addresses that are now to be made to His Majesty, for the security of religion, the union betwixt the kingdoms, and the peace and safety of the kingdom.

3. That he would strengthen and deliver our afflicted brethren in

England, who suffer by the violence and strange practices of the Sectaries.

4. That he would in his mercy prevent all these calamities and confusions that the present great revolution of affairs does threaten these kingdoms with, so hoping that you will be careful to stir up yourselves and others to wrestle with God in such an exigent, and to intimate the fast timeously, and to keep the same in yoiir several congregations the foresaid day. We shall only add that if there be any in your congregation who refuse to renew the Covenant, and are not excluded by the Act, our judgment is after you have convened them before you and found them obstinate, that you make public intimation of their names from your pulpits, as of persons who are disaffected and enemies.

to the cause of God, and that you refer them to the next General Assembly, till which time you are to suspend them from the sacrament of the Lord's Supper, and from all ecclesiastical charge, that so they may be in the same case with those who are excluded because of the malignancy and accession to the Engagement. We commend you to His grace, and rest

Your affectionate Brethren, The Commissioners of the General Assembly. Mr Robert Douglas, Moderator.

This interesting document is signed by one of the ablest leaders of the Church at this time. Mr Douglas preached the sermon previous to the coronation of Prince Charles by the Marquis of Argyll (January 1st, 1651).

April 14th, 1650. The Earl of Buchan was brought before the congregation this day for not signing the Solemn League and Covenant. James, Earl of Buchan, did stand up in his daske, and there declared before the whole congregation that he was sorry and grieved that he ever did adhere or have any dealing with those who went up to England in that unlawful Engagement. Also he did hold up his hand and sware to ye Covenant and subscribed it.

From the character of Buchan, he doubtless regarded the whole transaction as a fiasco, as most of the Cavaliers did. It was the dread of Argyll's "Act of Classes" which brought about his apparent contrition and submission, rather than the threats of minister and kirk-session, or regard for the Solemn League and Covenant.

April 23rd, 1650. Mr John Mignemane, chaplain to the Master of Gray, being appointed by Presbytery to preach in our church, refused and came not; so there was no preaching, because our minister preaching at Tealing, serving Mr John Campbell's edict.

This implies that the Presbytery of Dundee was split up into the two parties of the period viz., the Resolutioners and Protesters. The chaplain here referred to being a Resolutioner, would have no dealings with the Auchterhouse Protesters. The party spirit of the time precluded all ministerial and social intercourse.

April 23rd, 1650. Intimation was made from the pulpit forbidding all and every one in the parish to join with those rebels who were coming in the North, and that under the pain of excommunication.

The Marquis of Montrose while in the Low Countries was informed of the execution of the King. The intelligence so deeply moved him that he resolved to have revenge. Having met the young King at the Hague, preparations were at once made for fresh military movements in Scotland. A rising had already taken place in the North under Mackenzie a brother of the Earl of Seaforth James, Lord Ogilvy, Lord Eeay, c, who, with a body of clansmen, had fallen upon the garrison of Covenanters at Inverness. There was every expectation that the movement thus begun would spread throughout the Southern Highlands by the efforts of the disaffected Cavaliers. The intelligence also that Montrose had landed in Scotland created great alarm, so that the Covenanting party brought to bear all the terrors of the Church upon those likely to take up arms under him. In the edicts which were issued he is denounced as the excommunicated traitor, the unhappy and cursed man, James Graham, a child of the Devil, and as a man most justly, if ever any, cast out of the Church of God.

May 10th, 1650. James Swan and 'William "Watson are appointed to search alehouses in time of sermon. John Robertson and William Erskine are appointed by session against the next Sabbath to come before pulpit after they are called in and make their public repentance for going into England on that sinful and unlawful Engagement.

Tt is interesting to observe that the soldiers who had survived the Engagement and subsequent operations were now returning to the parish, and as they reappeared were summarily taken to task for their malignancy, and compelled to surrender and swear to the Covenant. It is quite evident the Royalist cause was wrecked, and the army well-nigh hroken up or disbanded.

May 20th, 1650. Intimation was made from pulpit of a thanksgiving to he kept on the 25th May, being Friday, for a victory obtained against the common enemy in the land; also, there were sundry papers read from the pulpit concerning a victory in the North, and of taking some prisoners.

Friday, May 25th, 1650. There was a thanksgiving kept for the victory the Lord hath given unto us in the North by overthrowing of our enemies, in putting them to flight, and in taking so many prisoners.

The Marquis of Montrose had landed in Orkney with a body of foreign auxiliaries to make one more attempt on behalf of the Steavarts, after the great reverse of Philiphaugh. The enterprise ruinously collapsed, as his forces were completely routed by Strachan's cavalry at Invercarron. After many adventures and hardships amid the Northern wilds and solitudes, he was driven to seek shelter from a former adherent, Macleod of Assynt. By Macleod he was made prisoner, and by General David Leslie's orders placed under escort to be taken to Edinburgh. On the way he passed through Dundee under a strong guard. By the inhabitants of the town he was received with marked respect and sympathy. His treatment was of a severe character on the march, for " he sat upon a little shelty horse without a saddle; but a quilt of rags and straw and pieces of ropes for stirrups, his feet fastened under the horse's belly with a tether, and a bit halter for a bridle, a ragged, old, dark reddish plaid, and a moutier cap upon his head, a musketeer on each side, and his fellow-prisoners on foot after him." He was delivered up to the Covenanting Government, and the sentence to be condemned, hanged, and quartered was carried out with barbarous severity. Thus terminated the strangely romantic and meteordike career of the great Marquis, the first historical personage of his day in Scotland, and, in the estimation of many, the solitary hero of his times. His personal appearance is thus described by Wishart: " He was not very tall, nor much exceeding a middle stature, but of an exceedingly strong composition of body and an incredible force, joined with an excellent proportion and fine features. His hair was of a dark-brown colour, his complexion sanguine, of a quick and piercing grey eye. He was a man of a very princely carriage and excellent address. He was a complete horseman, and had a singular grace in riding. He was of a most resolute and undaunted spirit." Although the most conspicuous figure throughout the civil Avar, the unflinching foe of the whole policy of Argyll and the ultra-Presbyterians, directly responsible for much of the misery and bloodshed which accompanied those unhappy times, besides unquestionably imbued with an unconquerable ambition, which to a great extent led him to attach himself to the reckless policy of the Stewarts, nevertheless Montrose possessed many qualities of an exceptionally high order. The resignation with which he confronted his melancholy fate; his heroism, noble bearing, and magnanimity, which truly shed a lustre over the dark scenes with which his stormy career terminated, have never failed to elicit the profoundest admiration. Unmoved by all the unpardonable insults and cruelties of vindictive partisans, he quitted himself like a man, and faced death with heroic fortitude. The night before his execution he inscribed the following lines with a diamond upon the window of his cell:

"Let them bestow on every airth a limb, Then open all my veins, that I may swim To Thee, my Maker, in that crimson lake; Then place my purboil'd head upon a stake, Scatter my ashes strew them in the air Lord! since Thou knowest where all these atoms are, I'm hopeful Thou'lt recover once my dust, And confident Thou'lt raise me with the just."

The capture of the great soldier who had so often, by his military exploits, filled the people with alarm, was, according to the custom of the period, followed by a thanksgiving service throughout the kingdom.

June 8th, 1050. It was condescended upon that there should be a school built for young ones.

June 19th, 1650. The minister forewarned all those who had not subscribed the Covenant that they should do it next Sabbath, and those Avho would not do that, that notice might be taken of them.

June 23rd, 1650. On that day there was intimation made out of pulpit for a fast to be kept on Sunday, 7th Juty.

July 1650. John Petrie and his wife Jean were before session for breaking of Sabbath day in fly ting and scolding each other, for which they were ordained to come before the pulpit next Sabbath, and make their public repentance and pay the penalty.

July 7th, 1650. In quoting from this record we shall adhere to the spelling of the 17th century.

On that day there vas a fast keepit. The cawses thereof are cawses of a publick aud solemne Humiliation appointed bee the Commissione of the Generall Assemblie to be keepit through all the congregations of the church, vpon the last day of June instant. Edinburgh, thee 21 of June 1650.

The Lord's dispensations hath often called this land to humiliation and fasting, sumtyms by the fear of snars, sumtyms by threatened violence, but the grounds of this holds foorth ane eminent degree of both these as a fruit of many misspent and abused solemne occasions; and although wee have no occasione to faint or cast away owr confidence in any difficultie, yet vee conceive it becoms all thee Lord's people throughout this Kingdome seriously to bee humbled for these cawses following: 1. The gryt danger the land and vork of reformation are into by the sudden and vnexpected approaching of the sectarean forces in our neighbour Kingdom of Ingland, vhich as it is vithout all cawse of provocation from vs, and inconsistent with thee oath of God in the Solemne League and Covenant and the large Treattie betwixt thee nations, so except the Lord prevent it, it threattns no lesse nor thee mine of this Kingdome and obstrowing of the vork of God vithin thee same.

Cromwell had now resolved to invade Scotland. Tin-invasion had been delayed and hostilities averted by the repudiation of the Engagement by the new administration. The young King having, however, landed in Scotland, the army of Cromwell advanced to drive him from the country, and to deal with the Scottish Covenanters, who were opposed to the execution of King Charles I. by the Republican leaders, and still maintained their sympathies for the fallen Monarchy.

2. The present distressed estat of thee people of God in Ingland, now groaning under the tirrany of that partie, vhich should the more affect us, seing, if Providence

doeth not othervayes dispose, ere long we ourselves may be browght to the lyk or vorse extremitie.

3. Besyd the danger vee ourselves are in besyd that partie from Ingland, vee are not vithout the reach of hazard from the malignant partie vhose inveterat malice against the work of God holds them on to persew the same des. ings hitherto by the blessing of God disappointed.

All those who had shared in the Engagement had either been suspended from church privileges or been excommunicated. Those who had refused to sign the Covenant or had broken their vows were recognised as enemies of the Reformation. This party was known by the designation of " Malignants," a term which frequently occurs throughout the proclamations of this exciting period.

4. Notwithstanding all the imminent dangers thee land layes in securitie, ignorance, profanitie, and formalitie litel conscience is made of the oath of God in our solemne vows, the guiltiness of shortcoming quharin and the breaches thereof before the Lord pleads against rulers, ministers, and souldiers, and people of all sort, besyd thee gryt vnthankfulnesse for mercies old and late, and the gryt abounding of sorcerie so common in many parts of this kingdome. We are therefore to pray 1. That God vould keep vs from thee danger of (the Sectarian army) drawing towards our border, that vee may neither bee infected bee their errors nor harmed by their violence, and that Hee vould disapoint all their designs against this land and the vorke of God, and brak the yoak from of the necks of his people in our neighbour Kingdome.

2. That Hee vould purge the land from profanitie, malignance, and all other sins, stire vp all sorts to their dutie, direct and blisse them in it, for thee furtherance of his vork and defence of his people, and that He may keep vs streight theirine that enemies get no advantage by our declyning from thee Covenant, either to the right band or to the left.

3. That Hee vould shew mercie to owr King, and cawse his vrath to cease from his father's house, and blesse the labours of our Commissionars vith him in bringing that treatie to such a solide close, as vee may be keeped from sin and snares, and hee brought to his throne, as may bee for the good of religione and comfort of his people.

In 1649, Commissioners had been despatched from Scotland to Holland to negotiate personally with the young King. No satisfactory terms could be effected with him, however, owing to the influence of Montrose, and others of the Cavalier and Malignant party. In 1650, Commissioners were again sent to Breda, and the young King at length agreed to accept the terms of the Covenanters. The defeat and capture of Montrose, and the hopelessness of raising a revolt in Scotland, brought about his surrender. Accompanied by the General Assembly's Commissioners, and a considerable number of worthless, dissolute old Cavaliers, he accordingly landed in Scotland on the 16th June 1650, near the Spey, and advanced to Stirling, where he was received by the leaders of the Scottish nobility.

4. That as hitherto the Lord has been ever for a defence to thee Assemblies of his Church, so hee vould be pleased graciously to countenance this insewing Generall Assemblie, both in the gathering and proceiding thereof.

28th July. On Sunday their vere intimatione made out of the pulpit of a fast to be keepit, the causes are these quilk vere continued in the last fast.

September 12th, 1650. At Stirling a solemne declaration and varning to all thee congregations of the Kirk of Scotland from the Commissione of the Generall Assemblie.

Albeit the Lord, vbose judgments are unsearchable, and vhose vays are past finding out, has brought the land verie low vnder thee hands of a prevailing enemie, yet most not vee bee silent to declare the mynd of God, nor others refuse to barken thereto; it ver sup superfluous to give answer to the many calumnies and reproches that wer layed abroad, for albeit in every thing vee cannot Justine the condine punishment of this armie, yet vee hold to our duetie not to believe groundlesse repentance, but rather to eye the Lord and to look to the hand that smytes them, and therefore in that pairt vee exhort and varne all the inhabitants in the land to search out their iniquities and to be humble before the Lord, that he may turne avay his wrath from vs. The Lord bath vounded and chastised us sore, quilk says that our iniquities are many and our sins are increased. It concerns the King to mourne for the preivous provocations of his father's house, for all his own guiltinesses, and to consider that if hee Kawe com vnto the Covenant and joyned himsellfe vnto the Lord upon polytike maters more for gaining himselfe a crown rather than to advance religione and right, that is ane iniquitie quhilk God vill not forget vnlesse it be speidily repented of. It concerns also ovr nobles and judges to try vhither their carriage in publick maters be streight and equall, or rather favour in seeking themselves and the things of this vorld, and how they valk in their privat conversationc. Their is in many a gryt dcale of pervernesse and incorigiblenesse in regaird of forsaken sume sins and performing surne dueties, notvithstanding publick professions and ingadgments, and this cannot but highlie provoke thee Lord; and it concerns the officers of the armie, especiallie these vho are chieffe among them, to veigh veill quhat the Lord has against them, and to repent of their diffidence and carnall vay of acting and vndervaluing of God's people; (the brethren) has also neid to search themselves and examine themselves as to their religious dueties, even anions; themselves there is much negligence and unfaithfulnesse to bee found, for which God is angry. Albeit the Lord has suffered that armie of perfidious and blasphemous sectaries to prevail, yet God forbid that thee land shovld complay vith them quhat ever may bee thee plausible and faire cariage of their land armie, yet doubtlesse their is a leaven of hospitalitie and error among them, all quilk the lowers of truth vowld avoid and discerne as thee Lord has tryed the stabilitie and integritie of his people in the land heirtofore by the prevayling of Sectaries, and soe vee trust that they vill think it their duetie and commendatione to prove sted-fast no less against the one than against the other. Neither void men be lesse cairfull and active in opposing this concerning than they have been in oposing Malignants heirtofore; our religione, liberties, and lyves are in as gryt hazard now aclayes as ever. All the ordinances of Jesus Christ are in danger, and the founda-tione lyke to bee overturned by these men who are obliest by these of them to maintaine all those. And it vere gryt guiltenesse to ly downne and crowch under the strange impossibilities they vould lay on vs, and as men vithout heart to suffer our land to be browght in bondage and our selves to bee robbed of all these things quilk are most precious and deare to vs. If vee void doe so, the Lord void be angry vith vs, and our posteritie void curse vs.

Yee void not think that all dangers from malignancie seeing their are a gryt many such vho yet returne their former principals, and therefore vee void vith as much vatchfulnesse and tender-nesse as ever avoid their snaris, and bevare of complying or conjuctions with them, and take head that vnder a pretence of doing for the cawse and for the King they get not power in to their hands for advancing and promoweing their old malignant desingis. Donbtlcsse, our saftie is to their first and former principalis, keiping a streight path vithout declining either to the reight hand or to the left. Secondly, it concerns all the inhabitants in the land to bee vare of murmuring and complaining against God's dispensations, and questioning the truth of our cawse, of quarrelling vith God, or bleaming or casting of the Covenant because of any thing that has befallen; that vere a gryt iniquitie not to be pardoned. Let vs beare the indignatione of the Lord. Mich 7. Postscrip.

It is also seriously desired that yee vil be instant vith God in your prayers, both privat and publick, that Hee void preserve us the ordinances of Jesus Christ, the kingdome. the King's Majesties persone, and the ministrie from the furie of this enemie, vho is seeking the overthrow of all.

This peculiarly vigorous and incisive proclamation was issued after the disastrous battle of Dunbar, fought on the 3rd September 1650, in which Cromwell completely defeated the Covenanting army under General David Leslie. The shattered Scottish army afterwards rallied at Stirling, from which town this proclamation was issued.

"Their vere sundrie Acts vreatin in another book, quilk ves taken away bee the enemie quhan they stormed the towne of Dundee."

This note is of considerable interest. It must have been made subsequent to this time, because Dundee was not stormed by Monk till August 1651. The book referred to may have been conveyed with other property, such as communion plate, for safety to Dundee, or it may have been removed during a raid of Monk's troopers. Most probably it was lost or destroyed during the siege. Everything of value was either destroyed or removed by the English soldiers at this time. The material collected within the town was immense, and the plunder was estimated by Balfour at above two millions and a half Scots. Monk's chaplain admits that it was " the best plunder that was gotten in the wars."

Sunday, September 22nd. Their vas a Fast keapit and Thursday following, the cawses are these following:

The cawses of a publicke humiliatione vpon the defat of our armie. Battle of Dunbar. Albeit solemne publicke humiliatione hawe been much slighted and gone about in a formal vay be many in this land, so that its not one of the least of our provocations that vee hawe drawen near vnto God vith our mowths, and keeped our harts fare avay from Him, for quhilk the Lord has turned the visdome of the vise unto foly and the strength of the strong vnto veaknesse; yet, seeing its a dutie that often lies proven comfortable to vs, and to quhilk now God calls us in a special vay by a singular peece of dispensatione, and knowing that all that are acquainted vith God vill make conscience of it, vee conceive its expedient that thee whole land bee humbled for these cawses following: 1. The continued ignorance and profanes of the whole body of the land, and the obstinacie and incorriglblenes of many, notwithstanding of the pains God has taken vpon us by His vord, and by His vorks of mercy and judgments to teach in the knowledge of His name and to informe vs of the evil of our vayes.

2. The manifold provocations of the King's howse, quhilk vee feare are not repented of nor forsaken bee him vnto this day, together vith the crooked and precipited vayes vhich vere taken by sundrie of the statsmen for caring on the treattie with the King.

3. The bringing home vith the King a gryt many malignants, and endevovring to keep svme of them about him, and many of them vithine the kingdome, notwithstanding of publick resolutions to the contrarie.

4. The not purging of the King's familie from malignant and profane men, and constituting the same of godly and veill affected persones, albeit it has been often pressed vpon the
Parliament and Committee of Estates and vndertaken and promised to bee performed by them.

5. The leawing of a most malignant and profane gaird of horse men to bee about the King, and vho being sent to bee purged, cam two dayes before the defatte, and were suffered to bee and feight in our armie.

6. The exceeding slacknesse of many, and aversnesse and untowardnesse of svme in the chieffe Judicatories in the kino–dome and in the armie in their conversations and publick dueties, especialle in these things quilk concern the purging of the Judicatories and of the armie from malignant and infamous persons, and filling all places of power and trust vith men of knawen integritie, and of blamelesse and Christian conversation (portion of MS. here obliterated).

7. The exceeding gryt diffidence of some of the chiefe of our armie and them among us vho thought vee could not be sawe (i. e., safe) but by a numberlesse armie, and vhen they had gotten many thousands together vowld not hazard anything, notwithstanding God afforded many faire opportunities and advantages, and fitted the spirits of the souldiers to duetie.

From this statement it appears that General David Leslie and the other Scottish officers were blamed for the defeat at Dunbar. It is well-known, however, that the battle was lost to the Covenanters by the incessant interference of the foolish and fanatical clergy who accompanied the army with the military tactics of Leslie. They refused to leave the camp; they even compelled him to dismiss a division of his best righting men simply because they were understood to be tainted with malignancy and other obnoxious qualities; they persistently harrassed him with their frivolous harangues, and were so clamorous in their demands for an immediate attack upon the enemy, that at length Leslie's attitude of caution and patience was abandoned. Leaving his commanding position, he executed that false movement which ultimately changed the fortunes of the war, and led Cromwell to say " Now the Lord hath delivered them into our hands."

8. The carnal confidence that was in many in the armie despising the enemie and promising the victorie to themselues without the eying of God.

9. The lowsnesse, insolencies, and oppressiones of many in the armie and the litle or no care that vas taken to helpe. the cawse, by quhilk it is come to passe that very much of the food of the poore people in the land has been needlessly destroyed. And virile vee remember of the profanitie and oppression of sundrie of our officers and

souldiers in Ingland, virile vee vere feighten for the Parliament in that Kingdome may not bee forgotten. Because, as it vas a gryt matter of stumbling to many in that land, so its lyk that it is one of thee cawses of the Lord's indignatione manifestit against vs by the hands of these men.

10. The our gryt vnthankfulnesse for many mercies and deliverances, and ewen for many tokens of the. Lord's fawoure and goodnesse tovards our armie virile they vere together, and the gryt impatience of spirit vliich vas to be seen in many these veeiks past, quhilk mad them limet the Lord, and to complaine and vearie of his delay to give deliverance.

11. The owning and eying the King's quarrel and interest in many vithout full consideratione to religione, and the libertie and savetie of these Kingdoms.

12. The carnal selfe-sceking and croked vayes of sundrie in our Judicatories or armies vho mak their places and employments rather a mater of increasing of fame and of preferment to themselves than of advancing of religione and righteousnesse in the land.

13. The not puting of difference betwixt these that served God and those that served Him not, for services or imployments accounting all men alike.

14. The exceeding gryt neglect that is in gryt ones and over many in performing in dewties in their famelies, notwithstand- ing of our former pleine acknowleging of this sin, as also thee neglect of the meanes of mutual edificatione, and our unfruitful-nesse and barrennes that is among all sorts of persons, vith a gryt deal of mixture of carnall securitie.

July 22nd, 1650. James Nickle gave in his bill of complaint against Margaret Tasker (his mother), following unto your Wisdome's humble means and complaints:

I, James Nickle, upon Margaret Tasker, who has calumniat me with her tongue by making me the father of ane lie in saying that I should say to My Lord and Lady Buchan that she had two sons wdio were abel soldiers for the wars. Also, she abused me with her tongue by banning and swearing and cursing, and saying that " bee God I leed, limmer"; so I humbly entreate your wisdome to do me reasonne.

This is a very amusing complaint made by a son against his mother, who, to judge from the record, was somewhat of a termagant. It is not recorded what punishment Margaret Tasker received. Most likely she would be cautioned to be more careful in the future, and not use such strong language to her highly-sensitive son James.

September 1st, 1650. The preparation sermon before Communion was preached by Mr William Japhray, Chaplain to Earl of Buchan. On that day the people were advertised to come at 10 hours in the morning.

This was the service held on Saturday previous to the Communion. Sacramental fasts were unknown at this time.

October 28th, 1650. John Monteith, James Christie, Thomas Mann, Burnhead; James Swan, Newton, were before session to undertake charge to be Elders and Deacons, which they consented to do, and the minister ordained them to be present on next Sabbath, 4 November, that they might give their oaths of fidelity before the whole congregation.

Nothing is said to imply that the elders of this period had to subscribe to any Confession of Faith. They were simply required to promise to act faithfully as parochial authorities, members of a church court, and administrators of discipline along with the minister.

November 12th, 1650. The minister did require at the elders at what time they thought fittest to examine the people, and that there was an Act of Assembly appointing minister to examine a day every week.

Thursday, November 14th, 1650. James Rodger, in Kirkton of Auchterhouse, being an elder in session, was discharged thereof by his own desire and by the consent of the session, because he could not conveniently keep the meeting, in respect be had none to govern his house and family except himself, for he had not a wife.

The minister warned people to go to the church of Lundie next Lord's Day, because he was to preach there. On that day a fast was kept, the causes thereof are as follows:

1. Because of malignity, deadness, lukewarmness of most pairts in respect of cause and work of God in this land, which makes us far short of that zeal and ferventness which becomes us, and which the Lord ought to have expected at our hands this day.

2. Because of a dead and lifeless ministry of late of the Lord's mercy discovered, which hath been the source and fountain of all our former evils.

3. Because of the desolate state and case of several large portions of the country being starved by dry-breasted ministers this long time byegone, and are now wandering like sheep without shepherds, and witnesseth no sense of scauth.

4. Because of the frequent scandal of witches and charmers in the part of the land, we are to supplicate the Lord that he would enlighten and incline ministers and people, and fill their hearts with more zeal to God and zeal to His truth, that the love of God may constrain us all to male more conscience of our engagments, and to pray that ministers and people may fall in love with Christ, and that more earnest desires may flow from wanting people for the means of their supply; and, finally, that the Lord would discover here all the work of Satan as he has begun to do in other places of the land, and bless all means that are and shall be for that effect.

November 18th, 1650. Isabel Petrie, in the Newtoun of Auchterhouse, was before the session for the breaking of the " glassin window" on that day the communion was given. When she was without in the kirkyaird sleeping her held fell through on the window and broke the glass.

Glass was most expensive and seldom used in those days. Windows were not generally made of glass, but were simply wooden shutters, which might be opened or shut when required. The "glassin window" was an important feature in the church, and the replacing of it must have been a serious matter for the unfortunate Isabel.

4th Sunday of December 1651. There was no preaching because of the storm of snow, and the kirk door could not be gotten open.

March 11th, 1652. The minister warned the people of Bal-beuchlie and Templeton to come at 10 hours to be examined.

May 2nd, 1652. Mrs Eobertson, in the Bonniton, was before the session for charming of her child, by going from the Bonniton to the Kirkton well and washing her daughter's eyes there, and saying:

"Fish beare fin and fulle beare gall, All ye ill of my bairn's eyen in ye wall fall."

The minister having heard her confession, found it necessary to take no action until he had brought her case before the Presbytery on the 22nd May.

Mrs Eobertson and Janet Fyffe, who had taught her how to charm the child, were appointed to sit on the stool of repentance, in sackcloth, ay till they be penitent.

July 18th, 1652. Janet Fyffe made her public repentance before the pulpit for learning Mrs Eobertson to charm her child, and whereas Mrs Eobertson should have done the same, it pleased the Lord before that time to call upon her by death.

Charming, like witchcraft, was one of the curious beliefs of this period. Every form of bodily and mental distress was generally ascribed by people, then so imbued with superstition and unlimited credulity, to the influence of evil spirits and certain diabolical agencies. The terror inspired by the Evil One was overpowering. For every ill that happened he was solely responsible. Moving to and fro in every conceivable form, all and sundry were at his mercy. Many remedies were discovered and reckoned to be thoroughly efficacious in charming away his wicked machinations. Many people had also profound confidence in the miracle-working power of certain old women in the country, whose advice was eagerly sought in all cases of bodily distress. Nothing could be done without solemn consultation with the local witches. No matter how absurd the prescriptions they recommended, they were at once complied with as infallible. Visits to sacred wells were in much favour, and during the washing process curious incantations were repeated, which were understood to promote resistance to the enemy, and the healing virtues of the well. At one time there was a strong superstitious belief in the healing properties of the Lady Well near the village. It had been formerly dedicated to the Virgin, hence its name. The well was situated at the north-east corner of the glebe, and there still exists an excellent spring at the same spot. It was alleged to have been much frequented in olden times by witches and charmers.

August 9th, 1652. It was disputed in the session whether the collections contributed at marriage should come to the box or to church officer, and the elders, with one consent, voted that the beadle should have it.

Collections for beadles at marriages long prevailed. When the practice of marrying in private dwellings became somewhat general, the minister was always accompanied by the beadle, for whose benefit a special collection was made by the company. This was in compensation for the loss of his fees through the breaking of the law.

Elders were enjoined to make strict search of alehouses on Sundays.

January 6th, 1653. The minister did intimate to session of two collections which are to be gathered the one for a prisoner, and the other for two men taken by Turks in toavn of Algiers.

Collections for all sorts and conditions of men were frequently made. The collection for prisoner doubtless refers to some victim of the civil war, and the other may be explained by the fact that the Mediterranean at this time swarmed with pirates, into whose hands Scottish merchants and sailors frequently fell. It was, however, not unusual for impostors to represent themselves as victims of the Turks, as it often proved efficacious in exacting sympathy.

June 13th, 1653. The session condescends that so soon as the minister gets money from my Lord Buchan to buy communion elements, he should delay no time in giving it.

This entry is of much importance, and clearly shows to what an absurd length the controversial spirit of the times had been carried. The church in 1651 had been rent by the violent conflicts between the Resolutioners and Protesters. After the battle of Dunbar, the party known henceforth as the Resolutioners wanted to modify or rescind the Act of Classes, and thus endeavour to unite the country and present a solid opposition to Cromwell. Their aim was to effect a compromise, and adopt a policy of expediency in the national crisis. The uncompromising Covenanters, henceforth known as Protesters, however, refused to come to terms with the Malignants. So strongly did feeling-run between the rival parties, that the communion was not observed for years in many parishes. The Protesters refused to sit down at the communion with any of the Malignants. Mr Wemyss, as a stubborn Covenanter and Protester, would have no communion celebrated, in which the Earl of Buchan and other parochial Malignants desired to join.

September 6th, 1653. Marjoria Thain and James Haliburton were before session for these speeches in saying that they would raise the Devill for the cloaths stolen from them if they got them not again. Confessing before the session, they were ordained to compeare before the Presbytery Wednesday come eight days.

September 13th, 1653. That day compeared Jean Vialant, in Rossie, before the session for taking upon her to reveal goods stolen by the airt that she had, and confessed that she got the ells of linen from Marjory Thain to dee the same. Being accused upon it, answered that ye woman blamed one James Halliburton, whom she would neither fyle nor cleange. Andrew Thain, in Kirkton, being present and examined as a witness, deponed in face of the session, and declared that he heard her say " By the knowledge that I have, and the airts that God has given me, that James Halliburton was the conveyer away of the goods." She is ordained to answer session by advertisement.

November 7th. That day James Halliburton made his public repentance before the congregation for those blasphemous speaches in saying that he would raise the Devill if he got not amends of Marjory Thain for alleging he was the conveyer away of her goods stolen from her.

In 1655, the Rev. Mr Wemyss, minister of the parish, died. From the numerous entries which occur in the parochial records during his ministry, he appears to have been a man of considerable zeal and energy. There is clear evidence also of the fact that he was a good example of the somewhat inquisitive, superstitious, and fanatical clergy of his age.

He was succeeded by the Rev. James Auchinleck, formerly of Kettins, on the 30th July 1656. While minister of Kettins he was brought before the General Assembly, upon an accusation of having been a defender of the doctrine of universal grace, but was acquitted of the charge of heresy.

The following entry regarding his appointment to this parish is of ecclesiastical interest, as it distinctly implies that the right of election of minister lay with the session, with the concurrence of the Presbytery:

Sunday, May 1st, 1656. Whilk day, after incalling of the nam of God bee Mr William Gray, minister at Fowlis, who haveing preached, and thereafter holden sessione, it being desired bee the said sessione that he should represent unto the Presbytery of Dundie their desir for obtaining the Presbytery's concurrence for planting a settled minister amongst them. After the said Mr William haveing taken the particular voices of everie one of the members of the said sessione did find that their desire vas to haue Mr James Auchinleck to be their settled minister, and vas thaireby desired bee the sessione to entreat the Presbytery to giue thair concurrence with the sessione to giue a call to the said Mr James. Lykas the sessione heirby bee their presents giues him a call, and does heirby commissionat David Rodger and Mester Alexander Ductor to goe alongs to the Presbytery for that effect. In vitness vbereof thair presents are subscribed bee the sessione day and place foresaid.

BUCHANNE.

Al. Ductor. By the Act of 1649, when any church -d tt became vacant, the Presbytery appointed one of their number to preach to the congregation and entreat the members to provide themselves with a qualified pastor. He was also instructed to signify that the Presbytery would send them preachers whom they might hear. Within a certain specified time the Presbytery sent one of their number to preach, and thereafter the session proceeded to elect a minister. If the people acquiesced and consented to this appointment, Commissioners proceeded to the Presbytery, intimated their choice, whereupon the Presbytery proceeded to admit him. If objections were lodged by the major part of the congregation against the appointment, and these were sustained by the Presbytery, a new election followed. Whenever a congregation was malignant, the Presbytery appointed the minister.

November 30th, 1656. There was an Act passed by the session that because some were importunate for baptism in forenoon, and the session finding that none of those people came back to afternoon sermon, it was ordained that none desire their children to be baptised before sermon unless they pay 30sh. The sacrament of baptism had to be administered in the face of the congregation, that what was spoken and done might be heard and seen of all, and administered after sermon, before the blessing. Private baptisms were and are still strictly opposed to the law of the church.

March 21st, 1658. The minister, the Rev. Mr Auchinleck, reported that the Presbytery had given commission to Mr William Gray and the minister to speak to my Lord and Lady Buchan anent their servant, Mrs Douglas, that they would cause her to attend God's service on the Lord's day, or else dismiss her. They promised to do so.

Nov. 2nd, 1662. Delated to the session, Patrick Gallants and David Smith, for their irreverent and scandalous carriage in the church by cursin' and fechtin' in time of service.

These two disturbers of divine service afterwards appeared and paid ilk ane o' them six shillings.

According to an Act of the reign of King James VI. all swearers of abominable oaths were to be fined and punished as follows: For the first fault, every prelate of kirk or lord, four shillings; a baron or beneficed man constituted in dignity ecclesiastical, twelve pennies; a landed man, freeholder, vassal, feuar, buyer, and small beneficed man, six pennies; the poor folks that have no gear, to be put in stocks, jougs, or imprisoned for the space of four hours; and women to be weighed and considered according to their blood, and estate of their parties they are coupled with. For the second fault, every prelate, earl, or lord, audit shillings; every baron or beneficed man in dignity, twa shillings; every landed man, vassal, feuar, and small beneficed man, twelve pennies; and every craftsman, yeoman, or servant, aucht pennies; the space of the poor folks' imprisonment to be doubled. For the third fault, the said second pains to be doubled; and for the fourth and last fault, the offenders to be banished, or put in ward for the space of a year and day, at the King's will.

It was also ordained that whatsoever person makes perturbation or impediment in the kirk, and will not desist therefrom, shall incur the pains as after follows: For the first fault, a prelate, earl, or lord, ten pound; a baron or person constituted in dignity ecclesiastical, five pound; a vassal, freeholder, burgess, or small beneficed man, forty shillings; and poor folks that have nae gudes to be put in prison for fifteen days, to fast on bread and water; and for the second fault the doubling thereof; and for the third fault, warding of their persons or banishing for year and day. Bairns that perturb the kirk to be leished.

In 1661 Episcopacy was re-established in Scotland. The Solemn League and Covenant, which had been accepted by King Charles II., 16th August 1650, was now repudiated by him on his restoration. It was declared to be illegal by Parliament, and copies of it were ordered to be burned. An absolute despotism and reign of terror followed. The King was declared by his minions supreme in all matters civil and ecclesiastical. All the laws in favour of civil liberty and the Presbyterian Church were swept away, in defiance of former solemn compacts, and the way accordingly made clear for a Prelatic ascendancy. The next step was the seizure, condemnation, and removal by execution of the great Argyll, and other distinguished Presbyterian leaders and preachers. A new Privy Council was created for the management of Scottish affairs, the most important of which was the carrying out of the King's resolution to interpose his Koyd authority for restoring the Church of Scotland to government by Bishops. Prelacy was thus proclaimed solely upon the authority of the King, notwith- standing all remonstrances. In the beginning of 1662, a proclamation was issued prohibiting all meetings of Synods, Presbyteries, and Sessions, unless by the orders of the newly-appointed Bishops. This was a greater blow than that inflicted in the reign of King James, for these courts continued to meet at that time, although presided over by a constant Moderator. Within a few months, by reason of such grossly unconstitutional and tyrannical enactments, nearly four hundred ministers were ejected from their livings. They were as speedily as possible replaced by Episcopalians, and from the testimony of one of their own Prelates, they were not generally a class of men likely to win the respect of their parishioners. According to Bishop Burnett, the new incumbents were generally very mean and despicable, the worst preachers he ever heard, ignorant to a reproach, many of them so openly vicious that they were a disgrace to their orders and the sacred functions, and in all respects simply the dregs and refuse of the Northern parts. This explains the Act of 1661, by which it was ordained that each minister who shall blaspheme, swear, or curse, or who shall drink to excess, shall be fined in the fifth part of his year's stipend. The dissolute and licentious character of many of the Prelatic presentees was at least well exemplified in the individual appointed to this parish as successor to the Rev. Mr Auchinleck.

June 15th, 1664. Mr James Campbell presented to the Presbytery a letter from the Bishop of Dunkeld for entering him on his trials in reference to the Church of Auchterhouse. The Presbyterie prescribed him a common heid.

On Mr Campbell passing his secondary trials before the Presbytery of Meigle, the Countess of Buchan (widow of the late Earl) sent a letter to them in December 1664, begging that the usual testimonial might be delayed. After being thrice in the pillare, and upon evident signs of his repentance, he was absolvit. He received his certificate on the 29th March, and was ordained 29th September.

December 1665. The Presbytery hearing that Mr James Campbell, minister at Aughterhouse, had fallen in fornication with dam Marjorie Ramsay, Countess of Buchan, did pas him thereanent, who confessed fornication with the Countess of Buchan, was humbled before his brethren, and was ordained to remove the scandal at Aughterhouse according to the order of the church, the whilk day the Presbytery did suspend Mr James until the next Synod of Dunkeld, having received a letter from the Right Reverend Father-in-God, Bishop of Dunkeld, his ordinal 1, to that effect, and inhibit the same Mr James to judgment the place of Aughterhouse. Mr James being asked by the Moderator, in name of his brethren, by whom and before which witnesses his child was baptised, answered that he baptised it himself in David Robertson's house, before those witnesses David Robertson, Helen Shepherd, and Margaret Grantur.

The Countess of Buchan being this day in Dundee, sent to the Presbytery humbly desiring that some of their number might be sent to her to take her confession, whereupon the Presbytery appointed Mr John Gourlay, Mr Robert Edward, Mr Thomas Ivinnear to go and take her confession, who, returning, reported that the Countess of Buchan confessed to them her scaudal of fornication, and s ibmitting herself to the church discipline.

Mr William Skinner appointed to preach at Auchterhouse the next day, and after sermon, before the blessing, to intimat Mr James Campbell his suspension from his ministry till the next synod of Dunkeld, and also to rebuke him publicly for his scandal of fornication from pulpit.

December. Mr William Skinner, Moderator of the Presbytery of Dundee, having preached, intimated to the congregation Mr James Campbell his suspension from serving the calling of the ministry till the Synod Assembly of Dundee, for one fornication committed betwixt him and dam Marjorie, Countess of Buchan, for the quhilk, by the said Presbytery's orders, he began his repentance on the pillare, sat both sermons, and is exhorted to repentance.

December 24th. Mr James Campbell for one fornication being thrice in the pillare, upon evident signs of his repentance was absolvit. In consequence of further misconduct he was suspended on his own confession till next Synod; but upon evident signs of his repentance he was absolvit from the pillare. Mr Andrew Oliphant is ordained to preach at Aughter-house upon Sabbath come 8 days, and to absolve Mr James Campbell. He thereupon retired from the charge. On the 14th February 1666 the church was proclaimed vacant.

December 21st. That dav the Countess of Buchan, for ane fornication committed with Mr James Campbell, her chaplain, began her repentance. Mr Andrew Evertis appointed to preach at Aughterhouse the last of December, and to rebuke the Countess of Buchan from the pulpit. Both were subsequently married, and, strange to say, Mr Campbell was appointed minister of Lundie, and what is also remarkable, the

Rev. John Robertson, M. A., minister of Lundie, became minister of this parish. It was simply an exchange of livings a singular arrangement, but one unfortunately too characteristic of such dissolute times.

May 3rd, 1665. A fast was intimated to be kept for the success of the Royal Navy.

July 5th, 1665. A public proclamation was read from the King's Majestie for keeping a day of solemn thanksgiving for the success of the Navy against the States Provinces.

On the 3rd June 1665, the Duke of York defeated the Dutch fleet off Harwich. Opdam, the Dutch Admiral, was blown up with all his crew. Eighteen of the enemy's ships were captured, and fourteen destroyed. This important victory, according to the custom of the period, was followed by a thanksgiving throughout the Church.

August 30th, 1665. A fast for the plague in England and for the harvest appointed to be kept on the 13th September.

This was the great Plague of London (1664-5) which carried off, it was estimated, nearly seventy thousand persons. Its terrible ravages created much consternation throughout the country, and a day of humiliation was appointed and subsequently observed. From what we know regarding the character of not a few of the Episcopalian incumbents, it is interesting to know that at a meeting of the Presbytery of Dundee, held on 15th September 1669, the brethren being severally removed, and inquiries made of their deportment in their charges and conversations, and whether they did preach twice on the Lord's Day and catechise weekly, and observe the Sacrament of the Lord's Supper once in the year, all were found faithful, approvehe, and encouraged.

April 27th, 1669. By the orders of the Presbytery of Dundee, action was ordered to be taken against all guilty of witchcraft. The Magistrates of Dundee were particularly desired to use all diligence for trying them further. They complied with the Presbytery's instructions, and appointed those suspected of witchcraft to be banished, " which was clone, and the Act put in execution."

The form of oath prescribed by the Presbytery during the Episcopalian regime was as follows: I, A. B., do acknowledge the present government of the Church of Archbishops and Bishops, and promise obedience thereunto, as witness my subscription.

June 10th, 1677. Delated to the session Andrew Ander-sone, Alexander Prowane, James Whittane, and Charles Jack, in Kirktowne, for not going to yee kirk yee preceding Sabbath, but staying at hame, and in time of divine service went to ye churchyard and plaid at ye pennie-stonne, and clam birds' nests. The parties compeared, and denied the charge the case deferred.

July 1st. The accused having compeared and confest their foresaid sinne of Sabbath-breaking, did humble themselves before the session for the samen, and they made publick satisfaction before the congregation. The game of pennie-stone or quoiting with stones was a favourite amusement in olden times.

August 5th, 1677. That day intimation of the communion to be given on Sunday next. The minister intreats because the giveing of the communion approacheth that the elders be carefull in their severall quarters to search who are at variance and discord with their neighbours, and aither reconcile them or els delait them to the session, to the end those who are contumasious and will not be reconciled may be debard from coming to the table of the Lord.

August 30th, 1677. The elders were desired to enquire and try in their severall quarters if there were anie who got tickets and examined and did not communicat, and delait them to the next dyet of session. The tickets referred to were tokens. The tokens in use at this time were small pieces of lead, unstamped and unmarked, about the size of a modern "sixpence."

September 9th, 1677. The Session finding that severall of the members of session keeps not the ordinarie meetings so punctual as it is requirit, but manie are found absent at the ordinarie tym of meiting, lies theirfor apointed that in all tym cuming non shal be absent from the session, but shall keep ordour, and everie absent shall be fynned in sex shilling Scots, except they can produce a verie lawfull excuse.

June 1684. Gilbert Millard and Elizabeth Hill were married. Witnesses William Clair, John Christie, James Webster, Alexander Bell.

July 11th, 1684. Alexander Bell and Christian M'Coan, both in this parish, were ecclesiastically contracted, and consigned their pledges conformable to church order.

Besides the payment for proclamation, consignation money had also to be tabled. This consignation money was a pledge that the purpose of marriage was bona-fide, and that the marriage would be solemnised according to the order of the church, at the proper time and place, after due proclamation of banns. If any impediment, scandal, or violation of the order of the church occurred, the consignation fees, which generally amounted to about o Scots, were forfeited, and lodged in the box for pious purposes.

July 26th, 1685. Janet Gowans compeared and gave satisfaction for her Sabbath breaking in shearing grass on the Sabbath day.

The Act of 1661 prohibited all salmond fishing, going of saltpans, milnes, or killes, all hiring of shearers, carrying of loads, keeping of mercats, or using any sorts of merchandise on the said day, and all other prophanation thereof whatsoever, under certain penalties. If unable to pay the penalties, the offender was to be exemplarly punished in his body.

The said day given to the Beddall for quarter fee, 17s. 4d.

August 1685. The Communion was publicly intimated by the minister to be given that day fortnight, and the elders were ordained to give a list of the names of those in the several quarters who bore at any time variance or discord among themselves.

It was the practice of the time to refuse communion to all who were understood to be quarrelsome and disorderly, and opposed to the reigning ecclesiastical authorities.

October 24th, 1685. This day being the King's birthday, it was solemnly kept. This was in obedience to a proclamation which was issued: " Forasmuch as it having pleased Almighty God to set our most rightful redoubted Sovereign, James VII. by the Grace of God of Scotland, England, France, and Ireland, defender of the faith, c, peaceably upon the throne of his Royal ancestors, our most august and glorious Monarch, notwithstanding the hellish plots and machinations against the sacred person of our late King (of ever blessed memory) and of our present Sovereign, whom God long preserve. Recommend to the Right Reverend the Archbishops and Bishops that they cause the ministers in their respective dioceses for this year, and yearly after, upon the said fourteenth of October, with the people at divine service in the church, devoutly to give solemn thanks to Almighty God, and celebrate His holy name for His so signal goodness and protection to our said gracious Sovereign, and in him to these kingdoms."

December 1685. Abraham and John Nicoll were delated to kirk-session for the sin of sacrilege in taking awa a daske from the church and breaking of it, and was ordained to be summoned by the session against the next day.

Abram Nicol compeared according to order, and denied he had any hand in that guilt at all, therefore he was desired to come next day and clear himself by his oath, which he refused. After much trouble he admitted he took the daske.

November 25, 1686. Mr John Eobertson, minister of Auchterhouse, had a lawful sun baptised by Mr David Ferguson, minister of Strathmartine, before the following witnesses "William Fullarton, John Nevay, David Crichton.

March 13, 1687. John Kendall, Abram Nicoll's servant, was appointed to be summoned against the next Lord's day for insolent behaviour in the bell-house on the Sabbath day.

March 27. John Kendall compeared before the congregation, and instead of satisfaction denied what he had confessed before the session the former Lord's day, wherefore the session decided to pass him as being ignorant of his duty both to God and man.

May 1, 1687. Which day the minister reported that the Bishop of Dunkell having drawn off from the Presbyterie of Dunkell all ministers belonging to the Diocese of Dunkell, and annexed them to the Presbyterie of Coupar in Angus, ordered all processes of complaints to be extracted out of the Presbyterie's Books of Dundie, and insert in the Presbyteries of Coupar, beginning quher before, c.

In 1687 King James II. issued his so-called "Indulgences," the most important of which was the third, in Avhich by his Sovereign authority, prerogative, royal and absolute power, he suspended all penal and sanguinary laws made against any for non-conformity to the religion established by law, granting to the Presbyterians leave to meet and serve God after their own way and manner, be it in private houses, chapels, or places purposely hired or built for that use, so that they take care that nothing be preached or taught among them which may any ways tend to alienate the hearts of our people from us or our government. This policy of granting toleration and liberty of conscience, although a welcome change from the protracted one of despotism and bloodshed, was in reality a stratagem for the removal of all restrictions against Popery, and, doubtless, it was further intended to create violent antagonism between the rival Protestant divisions. This indulgence was, however, to a large extent taken advantage of by the Presbyterians, who began to assemble together according to the old form of worship a privilege which was so long and ruthlessly denied them. Much dissension appears to have arisen in this parish, as in many others, during 1687, from sectarian enmity. Many disorderly scenes ensued, for the suppression of Avhich the minister and kirk-session seemed incompetent. The Rev. Mr Robertson appears also to have broken down in health, because the following entries occur in rapid succession: " No sermon in afternoon." " Minister very sick." " No sermon the minister not fully recovered." " The minister still sick," c.

January 1688. A proclamation was read from the pulpit against lying upon and scandalysing of Royal family. It was to the effect that none of the King's subjects shall presume to take upon hand, privately or publicly, in sermon, declamation, or familiar conferences, to utter any false, slanderous, or untrue speeches, to the disdain and reproach of his Majesty, his Council and proceedings, or to the dishonour, hurt, or prejudice of his Highness, his parents, and progenitors, or to meddle in the affairs of his Highness and his estate, present, bygone, and in time coming, under the pains contained in the Acts of Parliament.

Such proclamations, however, failed to prevent the Revolution from being consummated.

. May 1st, 1689. By order from Convention of Estates, there were two proclamations read that day the first ordering public prayers for King William and Queen Mary to be made, and the other for a voluntary collection for relief of Protestants who had fled out of France and Ireland into Scotland. The minister stated that he would collect it " att their dwellings."

The Eevolution was followed by a long and devastating civil war in Ireland. While the north of Ireland had declared for King William, the greater portion of the country still remained loyal to James. The province of Ulster was overrun by the army of Tyrconnel, and conflicts of the most sanguinary character embittered by the old race animosities ensued between the rival religionists, in which the Protestants suffered severely. Those who escaped the sword fled into Scotland, and everything was done by their Presbyterian brethren to alleviate their sufferings.

The collection was also in behalf of French Protestant refugees driven from France by the Revocation of the Edict of Nantes.

In 1689, the English Convention declared that James II., having endeavoured to subvert the constitution of the kingdom by breaking the original contract between the King and the people, and, by the advice of the Jesuits and other wicked persons, having violated the fundamental laws, and withdrawn himself out of his kingdom, has abdicated the government, and the throne is become vacant. The vacant throne was given to the Prince and Princess of Orange as joint Sovereigns. The King and Queen were shortly afterwards proclaimed publicly in Edinburgh. During this memorable and exciting period, Dundee and the southern portion of Angus were overawed by the notorious Graham of Claverhouse, who, at the head of a considerable body of retainers, had taken up a position in the Glen of Ogilvy, from which he descended on one occasion and destroyed out of revenge the Hilltown of Dundee. As Viscount Dundee and Constable of the Town titles bestowed upon him for his services against the Covenanters he wielded considerable influence, and with characteristic vigour did his utmost to maintain the Royal authority, and preserve Prelatic supremacy throughout Angus.

On the 13th April 1689 a proclamation was issued by the Convention of Estates appointing public prayers for King William and Mary, with certification that those who refused should be deprived of their benefices. On the 22nd July an Act was passed abolishing Prelacy, and declaring the re-establishment of Presbyterianism. The Revolution Settlement was naturally received with violent opposition by the Prelatic clergy of Angs, who were entirely in favour of the dethroned Sovereign. Supported as they were by the Jacobite nobility and gentry, they presented a formidable opposition. A great number of the clergy refused to conform to Presbyterianism. From the records of the Privy Council, there were altogether two hundred and two offenders against the proclamation. The majority of these offenders were, however, permitted to remain in possession of their benefices and emoluments if they chose to do so. In parishes vacated by the Episcopal curates, efforts were at once made to replace them by Presbyterians. The General Assembly, however, was allowed to try and purge out all insufficient, negligent, scandalous, and erroneous ministers by due course of ecclesiastical proofs and censures.

In 1690, a Commission was granted for visitation on the north side of the Tay, and instructed to admit to ministerial communion and a share of the government such of the Episcopal clergy as they on due trial found to be orthodox in doctrine, of competent abilities, having a pious, godly, loyal, and peaceable conversation, of an edifying gift, and who they believe should be true and faithful to God and the Government, and diligent in their ministerial duties, that shall subscribe to the Confession of Faith, and profess their submission to and willingness to join and concur with the Presbyterian Church government.

This Royal policy of extreme moderation and leniency toward the Prelatic incumbents was deeply resented by the faithful Presbyterians. They completely failed to see how men who had striven to wreck Presbyterianism, and were so closely identified with a former bloody, merciless, and intolerant regime, should be received into the bosom of the Church on terms so easy and favourable. This was certainly a breadth of toleration marvellous in their eyes, fiu. n the fact that such a thing was unknown under the old ascendancy from 1661-1690. Their admission was not only a blunder, it was a crime. The whole policy was believed to be suicidal, utterly void of principle, and destructive to the vital interests of the Church. No doubt these incumbents professed to have signed the Confession of Faith, and had apparently embraced Presbyterianism; but the Presbyterians had very strong reasons for believing that they were not sincere disciples of the real old true-blue form of worship and government. They were to all intents and purposes still Prelatic in their opinions, and active agents of the Jacobite party.-

In 1690 a considerable number of the worthless incumbents were Aveeded out on the score of immorality, but very few because of Episcopal proclivities.

In 1691 strong efforts were made by the Prelatic party to regain their position. They urged their demands upon the King most persistently, but he refused to listen to their overtures.

For many years, therefore, the service was conducted very much as formerly, particularly throughout the Northern counties, Avhere the Jacobite and Prelatic influence was all-powerful. Very frequently, when an attempt was made to conduct service according to the instruction sent down by the General Assembly, riotous mobs assembled, acting under the instigation of the Jacobite lairds. They did everything possible to prevent the Presbyterian service being held, and did not even hesitate to attack the minister, and those who supported him, if they showed a disposition to conform to the government and discipline of the church. In this neighbourhood violent and disgraceful attempts were made by hired ruffians to prevent the re-establishment of Presbyterianism.

May 12, 1689. Intimation was made that there was a thanksgiving to be kept on Thursday next, being 16th, for a deliverance from Popery.

Thursday, 16. On that day thanksgiving was kept and sermon preached.

June 16, 1689. John Hill having gotten 5 4s. of doites out of the box to exchange, gave back 2 10s. of good turners gotten for them, and it was imboxed.

A great weakness in olden times was the persistent dropping of bad coins into the collecting ladles. Sales of bad coins repeatedly took place; but such coins never seem to have disappeared. Foreign coins also were in great favour, and found their way into the box in great numbers. Doites were Dutch coins, and in value nearly equivalent to a penny Scots. From the close relationship between Scotland and Holland, the coinage of the latter country was very plentiful in Scotland. Turners were two penny pieces of Scots money. Notwithstanding the vigilance of elders, the surreptitious passing of such coins into the brods long prevailed.

July 7th, 1689. That day the minister produced the Moderator's discharge for the 12 17s. 8d. collected for the French and Irish Protestants, and it was imboxed.

October 1689. John Liddel compeared before session for his righting on the Sabbath day, and striking John Bell. He confessed with humiliation before the session and was absolvit.

November 1689. John Marr was in the place of repentance, and was spoken to by the minister. On evidence of his repentance, absolvit and paid his penalty, 4.

November 1689.

Given to John Hill to buy the poor folks shoes, 4 0 0

To J. Roger, to buy him shoes, 0 10 4

To William Jack, to buy him shoes,. 0 10 0

To Mary Jack, to buy her shoes, 0 18 0

To Agnes Roger, to buy her shoes, 0 IS 0

November 24th. Peter Bruce supplicated the session for help. In regard he was become, weak by age and disease, the session promised him 8s., and to relieve him in future as his case required.

July 1st, 1690. This day the fast was kept according to the former intimation, and according to proclamation on the Sunday before, in name of the King and Queen, for the distress in Ireland, for the preservation of the King's person, and success to his armies and fleet. Collection taken, 9s. It was given to beadle out of goodwill.

August 3rd, 1690. Thanksgiving kept for victory obtained in Ireland, and for the preservation of the King's person.

This was the battle of the Boyne, in which King William defeated his father-in-law, James II., 1st July, 1690. James fled to Dublin, thence to Waterford, and made his escape to France.

May 1st, 1691. Proclamation was read for keeping a fast every last Wednesday of May. June, July, and August, for preservation of their Majesties' persons, and success to their armies and fleets in defence of Protestant religion.

July 19th, 1691. That day it was enacted that the elders who gather the offering shall survey the change-houses in time of sermon. Of the scandalous persons only Thomas Robertson compeared, but refused to pay his mulct or satisfy penalties, and appointed to appear in public the next Lord's day, and is ordered to speak to the minister on Sunday before his appearance. William Wallace had promised to come and make his public satisfaction, and came not. The minister promised to speak to the minister of Strathmartine anent James Angus, if he would cause him to come and make satisfaction for his Sabbath drunkenness and tulzing. He afterwards came and satisfied by fine of 13sh.

October 1692. Given out to Dauvit Wyddie, for girding the barrell that holds the Communion wine, 3d.

This is a somewhat quaint entry, and refers to times which belong completely to the past. On Communion occasions great quantities of wine were used generally light claret or

Burgundy. Indeed, it is somewhat perplexing to know how such quantities as are entered in the records could ever have been made use of.

The system of partaking of the wine must have been entirely different from that of modern days. There are also entries showing that certain individuals received money for bringing " oot the barrell from the toon." For many years Communions must have been conducted in a very primitive way in this parish. When the old pulpit was being removed some years ago we were a little startled to discover beneath it a recess which contained a well-constructed case, with sub-divisions capable of holding a considerable number of bottles. This must have been the wine-cellar which succeeded the decayed barrel. Entrance to this curious cellar was by a small door somewhat concealed by the precentor's box.

October 1692. No sermon to-day, being stormy. This entry is repeated frequently throughout the close of this year.

Thursday. The thanksgiving was kept for the King's safe return to London. No collection, from the paucity of people.

February 1694. In regard Patrick Ogilvie hath borne the burden of David Edieman, his father-in-law, for some years bye gone, and that he was unable for work, therefore the session determined that he should paj r nothing for the mort-cloth at his burial, he being in a mean condition.

Where no parish bier or coffin existed it was quite usual, at one time, at the burial of the poor, to use a sheet called the mortcloth, in which the corpse was wrapped on the way to the place of burial. The body was then taken out and lowered into the grave by ropes. This was the origin of the parish mortcloths, those elaborate coverings made of velvet, with fringes. These were kept by the kirk-sessions, and hired out according to fixed charges to parishioners and others. No burial at this time was considered to be properly conducted without the mortcloth. The charge at this time was 10s. The fees exacted for the mortcloth were very considerable, and went to the box.

In 1695 an Act was passed that an elder or deacon should he present at the coffin-ings. Wakes or lykewakes were the custom of the period, and were largely attended. The elder was appointed simply to maintain order, as riotous and drunken scenes were too common on such occasions. During the coffining and subsequent funeral services, there was frequently more tobacco and drink consumed than on many marriage occasions. Great crowds assembled, and were drawn together very much by the prospect of ample smoking, feasting, and drinking. The foolish notion of the age was that no funeral was heartily conducted without guzzling and immoderate drinking, followed by a plentiful supply of pipes and tobacco. The funeral customs in olden times were in many respects very objectionahle.

At this time many curious entries occur:

To Thomas Croall, for transporting a gentlewoman from this place to Strathmartine,. To David Roger, being sicker than ordinar,. To certain poor gentlemen, To distressed gentlemen, To ane Mackintosh, a gentleman, To Elizabeth Campbell, a minister's relict,.

The distress throughout the country at this time seems to have been very great. Parishes appear to have been invaded by beggars from all quarters. The petitions for relief from the box were frequent, and many of them from people at one time apparently in better circumstances. From the records we can quite understand that there must have been a certain amount of truth in Fletcher's description of the times. " There are," he says, " at this day in Scotland (besides a great number of families very meanly provided for by the church boxes, with others who, with living upon bad food, fall into various diseases), 200,000 people begging from door to door. At country weddings, markets, burials, and other the like public occasions, they arc to be seen, both men and women, perpetually drunk, cursing, blaspheming, and fighting together."

The last Episcopal clergyman of the parish was the Rev. Andrew Bissett. He succeeded Mr Robertson in 1688. For many years his bible, a large folio volume, strongly bound in oak, was preserved in the parish. It bore the following quaint inscription, written in the cramped style of writing peculiar to the period:

"Andrew Bisset, his book,

Ye living Lord upon him look; And when ye bell begins to tolle, Ye Lord haue mercy on his soule."

On November 1st, 16'J9, the Laird of Auchterhouse, Patrick Lyon, a well-known Jacobite, petitioned the Presbytery that they would delay declaring the parish vacant. The Presbytery, however, declined to listen to his petition. It was the laird's wish, apparently, that the parish should remain Prelatic.

March 6th, 1700. This day, several of the parish of Auchterhouse having compeared and presented to the Presbytery a call to Mr Thomas Fraser, preacher of the Gospel, desiring their concurrence in order to Mr Fraser being settled among them as their minister, which the Presbytery finding weighty, they told the said pecple of Auchterhouse that in regard of some Act of the General Assembly they could not proceed in their affair till they had advice from the Commission of the General Assembly.

March 20th. The which day compeared Mr William Crichton of Adamstone, and produced his commission from the parish, impowering him to demand of the Presbytery that one of the ministers lie sent to moderate in a call to Mr Thomas Eraser to be their minister, in order to the making up of the formality which was wanting in the former, and produced an Act of the Commission advising the Presbytery, as they see cause, to proceed in the said affair: Whereupon the Presbytery, having taken U consideration the whole affair, completely found that they could not grant the said desire in regard of the. repeated Arts of the General Assembly anent those who have the Irish language, and an appointment of the late Assembly, as likewise the disatisfae-tion of the generality of the members with the person called, and therefore refuse their concurrence in this affair. Against this decision an appeal was taken to the Synod. An inquiry followed. A Professor of Divinity connected with the Presbytery (if Ross gave his opinion regarding Mr Fraser in the following quaint and sarcastic terms. He stated that Mr Fraser was too well-known all this country over, particularly to the members of the Presb r tery, to have more sail than ballast, and since this impression is confirmed by several things which have been talked of him, we are very adverse from calling him among us; but if the tossings and harrassings which he has of late suffered before the Judicatories of the Church, both south and north, have made him low his sails and humble himself before the Lord; if he has been made to cry to Heaven for ballast and received it, and that to the conviction and satisfaction of the Reverend Presbytery of Dundee, among whom we hear he is for present resides, and if after a year's stay among them, and received confirmations of spiritual ballast (natural and intellectual ballast we do not expect that he ever shall exceed in it, but grace may act pleasantly on the weaknesse of nature), received by the said Mr Thomas, and discovered by that Reverend Presbytery; if thereafter they make an offer of him to us, we shall think of it, and reckon it an argument of self-denial in them and great sympathy with us. The Earl of Strathmore and the Laird of Auchterhouse having, however, also refused to concur in such a call, the case was referred to the Commission of the General Assembly, who put it aside. Mr Fraser accordingly was compelled to seek some other sphere of usefulness.

The long and deplorable reign of Episcopacy at length came to an end, notwithstanding much opposition on the part of the laird and principal heritors. Had the Presbytery, however, not interfered, it would most undoubtedly have continued. This shows the remarkable hold the Jacobites had of the parish, and the keenness manifested by the Episcopalians to keep possession.

It was now nearly twelve years since the Eevolution settlement, and as yet there had been no real recognition of Presbyterianism.

The Eev. Patrick Johnstone was appointed minister of the Parish in 1702. He was called by the Presbytery jure devoluto 16th September, and ordained 29th December 1702. The Presbyterian discipline and government being now supreme, the greatest possible care was exercised in the appointment of ministers. Strict inquiry was made into their piety, gravity, prudence, sobriety, orthodoxy, and learning. All who were considered vain, imprudent, proud, worldly-minded by the generality of sober, intelligent persons, were ordered to be kept back. All ministers were instructed freely and faithfully to preach against the enormous sins of profane and idle swearing, cursing, Sabbath-breaking, profane withdrawing from and contempt of gospel ordinances, fornication, adultery, drunkenness, excessive tippling, deism, blasphemy, and other gross and abominable sins. They were beseeched, exhorted, and required to take heed to themselves and the doctrine, to be strict in catechising, to be careful in dealing with heads of families, to engage persons of honour to fall in love with holiness, to keep a very watchful eye on Papists, to suppress all heresies and books freighted with impious, pernicious, and siml-destroying doctrines, and verv curiouslv to seek to reclaim all Quakers from their abominable heresies. It was a time of great strictness, and the penalties enacted were heavy for any infringement of the law. A revival of the old Puritan discipline ensued.

There was not even the shadow of toleration shown towards offenders. All kinds of cases came up before the session. Nothing was too trivial to be dealt with if duly reported. The cases investigated and gravely considered were of as miscellaneous aud disreputable a character as appear before the modern police courts. The minister and kirk-session were supreme, and a terror to evil doers. The beadle's duties were of an onerous character, and the opportunities afforded him of introducing culprits to their judges were by no means few and far between.

Every case, no matter how delicate, was sifted to its foundation by the summoning of witnesses and other formalities. One marked feature in the administration of discipline was the granting of the Oath of Purgation. When any grave scandal was brought against a member of the church, and strongly denied by him, he was permitted, in certain circumstances, to clear himself by taking this oath. Its terms were certainly of a character to strike terror into the most hardened, and clearly imply that lying and perjury were of little moment in those rude and licentious times. The following is the Oath of Purgation jnven in the Form of Process of 1707: " I, A. P., now under process before the Presbytery of., for the sin of., alleged to be committed by me, and lying under that grievous slander, being repute as one guilty of that sin, I, for ending of the said process and giving satisfaction to all good people, do declare before God and this. that I am innocent and free of the said sin., and hereby call the great God, the Judge and Avenger of all falsehood, to be witness and judge against me in this matter if I be guilty; and this I do by taking His blessed name in my mouth, and swearing by Him who is the Great Judge, Punisher, and Avenger as said is, and that in the sincerity of my heart, according to the truth of the matter and mine own conscience, as shall answer to God in the last and U'reat day when I shall stand before Him to answer for all that I do in the flesh, and as I would partake of His glory in heaven after this life is at an end." Solemn as this oath is, it is certainly more mildly expressed than is the case in many other oaths administered before this time. They are throughout painfully extravagant, unseemly, and discreditable to those who exercised them.

The old strictness in the granting of testimonials to parties moving from one parish to another was also revived. Many of those testimonials were of a very quaint description. As a rule, they were written upon long narrow strips of paper, and entered most minutely into the character of the individuals to whom they were granted. The minister, accordingly, had no difficulty in knowing the true ecclesiastical position of his new parishioners. In the event of any misdeeds being recorded against them, these were carefully and minutely stated. Be it known that A. B. is a (then follows the particular appellation). Many of the parishioners in those days must have opened their eyes at the harsh revival of old sores, and the minister's wonderful acquaintance with many shortcomings in rural life, which they never for a moment dreamt he was cognisant of. An important feature of the period was the great attendances upon communion occasions. Those sacred seasons were viewed as yearly reunions of friends, and were characterised by much excitement. People nocked from other parishes provided witli their tickets or tokens to admit them to the table. The usual custom was to have a tent pitched in the churchyard for the sale of ale, c. Such gatherings were by no means so conducive to parochial morality as they ought to have been, as the day too often terminated in boisterous scenes within the village alehouses.

In 1706, an Act was passed appointing a national fast for the purpose of supplicating the divine direction respecting the Treaty of Union, on the consideration of which the nation was about to enter. On the 13th October the Scottish Parliament met, and an Act of Security was passed in which the Acts confirming the Confession of Faith and the Presbyterian form of Church government were ratified and established, to continue without any alteration to the people of this land in all succeeding generations, and it was further declared that this Act of Security with the establishment therein contained shall be held and observed in all time coming as a fundamental and essential condition of any Treaty of Union to be concluded betwixt the two Kingdoms, without any alteration thereof or derogation thereto, or any sort for ever. The Act of Security was therefore the basis of the Act of Union, and the Church of Sent land was placed on a secure foundation. The Articles of Union, after being accepted and ratified by the English Parliament, were returned to Scotland, and registered by the Scottish Parliament, 25th March 1707.

In 1708, a solemn thanksgiving was observed for the Nation's deliverance from the Pretender.

In 1713, an address was ordered to be read from all the pulpits warning the nation against the designs of the Jacobites, who were now Avorking steadily for the Pretender.

After the death of Queen Anne, on 1st August 1714, there was great excitement throughout Angus, which culminated on the proclamation of George as King. Strathmore being the centre of Mar's rising in favour of the Cbevalier, much excitement and serious riots took place in several parishes, and mobs were collected to attack the Presbyterian clergy and their people. The Battle of Sheriffmuir, however, terminated such disorders, and in a short time the storm had disappeared.

Mr Johnstone died on 2nd May 1740, after a ministry of thirty-eight years. The initials P. I., A. D. 1726, still remain upon one of the manse walls. He was succeeded b r the Rev. James Scott. In 1775, the church was to some extent altered and entirely reseated. The manse Avas built in 1789, at a cost of 322 losh. Scot. Some of the entries of this period are of a very quaint character.

As it has formerly been a practice in the parish to give the church officer as much corn as each person may think fit, the kirk-session of Auchterhouse hope that all to whom he may apply will contribute according to their generosity. Occasional sales of wood were also conducted under the auspices of the session, intimation of which was made by the beadle on Sundays from a prominent gravestone in the churchyard. Certain regulations were carefully drawn up for such occasions.

1. The highest bidder is always to be preferred, upon the judges pronouncing the word "thrice."
2. Credit to be given upon such security as shall satisfy the offerers.
3. Each bode must exceed the former by one penie.
4. All below a croon must be ready money.
5. C. J. is constituted baillie to said roup.
6. The cryer must have the ordinary dues.

Some of the accounts are also of a very quaint character:

To the surgeon for amputating a man's legg, The mixtures to him,. The powders to him,. The cordial mixture to him,
The ointment to him,. The ditto to him,. The eerat to him,. To a timber legg to him,. To leathers and buckles to the leg". To twenty-two horse hires to him,

This surgical operation, c, cost 142 losh., for which there was a special collection made throughout the Presbytery.

During Mr Scott's ministry, and for many years afterwards, the parish was notorious for the extent to which the pernicious system of smuggling in whisky was carried on. From the well-wooded and hilly character of the district, which afforded ample concealment, and, at the same time, from its easy access to Dundee, which was always ready for a good supply of the homemade article, the traffic was carried on by old and young to an extent which is hardly credible. Everything was done by law to suppress it, but, still it continued to increase. By an Act of Parliament of 1719, all ministers were strictly enjoined to represent to their people and hearers the great impiety and monstrous wickedness of such methods to gain the world, to the endangering of their souls, and earnestly to obter them to abstain from such crying sins and deadly courses. Similar Acts followed in 1736 and 1744. The whisky was brought from Glenisla and other well-known haunts of smugglers across the hills, by means of double ankers slung over the backs of Highland ponies. In those days it was quite an everyday occurrence to witness a procession of smugglers marching along with their ponies each pony being secured to the tail of the one in front by moans of a halter, while alongside marched the stalwart Highlandmon, armed with thick bludgeons to cope with any opposition from the revenue officers. When they reached the parish by the hill bridle path, they found themselves in comparative safety, for within it there were many who had good-going stills of their own, and whose chief business was that of running the whisky into town. The whisky was either sold on the spot by the smugglers to their country customers, or carefully guarded until a favourable opportunity presented itself of having it conveyed to Dundee in safety. In cases of probable capture by a strong body of excisemen when en route, the ankers were in a twinkling unslung, hurriedly concealed in the heather or buried in the moss, while the smugglers mounted the backs of their nags, and soon were out of reach of the enemy. Few could excel the smugglers within the parish for ingenuity in cheating the gangers, and had the recipients of the liquor in town only known by what means it was too frequently conveyed for their benefit, they would most assuredly have hesitated to swallow it Opinion appears to have been somewhat divided as to the quality of the article. We have heard it described as " coorse drink," " pushion," c.; while others, who might be recognised as fair authorities, with a hearty chuckle, broad grin, and pawky shake of the head, have extolled its merits as " graun whusky jist." Many amusing-stories might be related of those days. A man belonging to the parish was on one occasion on his way to Dundee with a sack on his hack which contained several bladder skins filled with whisky. While bearing along his precious burden with a refreshingly innocent expression, he was suddenly confronted by a very shrewd gauger. Taking in the situation at once, the guager quietly took out his pocket knife, administered a few sharp probes into each of the skins, and told the man to run for his life, which he did as rapidly as his legs could carry him. The humour of the transaction may be imagined. Great fertility of resource was also shown in concealing the ankers. When the alarm was raised that the enemy was approaching, all hands set to work, and in a few minutes, as if by magic, the ankers disappeared under manure heaps, and other primitive rustic hiding-places.

On one occasion, while troopers were going their rounds in search of smugglers and ankers, they were seen to approach the house of one of the principal farmers in the parish. This visit evidently meant business, and was likely to prove somewhat unpleasant for the farmer, who was perfectly aware of the fact that a considerable quantity had been recently stored away within his premises. With great good humour and perfect coolness, he met the troopers when they drew up at his door, and said to them " Come awa in, lads, come awa," which they accordingly did. Refreshments were at once produced, and a good supply of the very best of the " smuggled" was passed round and much enjoyed. While the troopers were thus being entertained by the farmer, his servants were at the same time actively engaged in getting the ankers out of the premises into a place of greater security. A ery frequently desperate encounters ensued between the excisemen and smugglers, and blood was even shed over the struggle for the possession of the ankers. The following account of one of those fights shows the extent of the traffic, and the troubles connected with it:

March 12th, 1813. On Friday last, Mr John Black and Mr Thomas Lowson, excise officers in Dundee, assisted by another person, seized in a field to the north of Auchterhouse nine and a-half ankers of Highland whisky, consisting of 95 gallons. They put it in a cart, and were three or four miles on their road to Dundee, when they were furiously attacked by three Highland-men with sticks and stones. A desperate combat ensued, and continued for an hour, when both parties were much hurt. ne of the smugglers received a shot in the neck from one of the officers, and one of the officers received two severe cuts in his head from the smugglers. During the scuffle, the smugglers abstracted three and a-half ankers from the cart, and hid them in the plantation at the side of the road, but the officers brought off the other six, and lodged them in the excise office, Dundee. It is said that while the officers of excise and the smugglers were engaged some farmers passed by, but refused to give any assistance. The traffic was only suppressed by the employment of mounted troopers, who proved too strong and vigilant for the Highlanders continuing the traffic with any reasonable success or profit. Although for years afterwards an occasional gallon was made, " jist oot of sport," for home consumption, the practice so long stubbornly maintained died away. The worm of an old still the last of its race, doubtless, within the parish, and which, apparently, had seen much service in its day and generation was recently presented to the Society of Antiquaries.

The records of the eighteenth century also contain material of some interest, but of a character almost entirely local. It is interesting to observe the dawning of better times, and the old stern system of discipline gradually wearing into milder and more seemly methods of enforcing ecclesiastical authority. At times there are outbreaks of scandal, and an occasional fight in the church occurs. A decided improvement in tone and morale, however, becomes distinctly perceptible, notwithstanding such incidents. The records are. occasionally varied with entries regarding important victories by sea and land, and the appointment of thanksgivings for the same. It is surprising how much information may be gleaned from these old parochial records. Not only are they valuable to the ecclesiastical antiquarian, but to all who are in any way interested in the quaint transactions within the Scottish Church in former times. However dull, tedious, and uninteresting it may seem to many to carry research into old, musty, and well-nigh illegible parochial records, still one is often rewarded by information of a most valuable and instructive character, for it must be remembered that such documents were among the most important of their day in the country, and in many cases form the sole repositories of former ecclesiastical life and authority. These records carry us back to times when the Church was the great centre of parochial life, and in every respect supreme. They take us completely behind the scenes; they tell us graphically many a strange, quaint, droll story; they give us complete photographs of much original character; they throw wonderful light upon the moral and social condition of the people; they afford us such insight into the real life of the country as we can find nowhere else; they bring to the surface many remarkably curious and venerable phases of thought; and, above all, they show what marvellous progress this country has made in all departments of social, spiritual, and intellectual life.

The Kev. James Scott, who wrote the statistical account of the parish in 179-'), says: "There are 12 farmers, 40 weavers, 7 wrights, 2 smiths, 2 tailors, 8 dikers, G quarriers, 2 shoemakers, 3 merchants' small shops, 3 retailers of ale and spirits. 1 clergyman, 1 schoolmaster. Xo lawyer, writer, doctor, surgeon, apothecary, butcher, baker, brewer. Rheumatism, scrofula, and smallpox arc common."' In 1775 no less than 20 died from smallpox in the space of six weeks. He says he could not get the people to inoculate their children. They always said: " To inflict a disease is tempting Providence." In the parish he states there were 5 bridges, 2 corn mills, 1 lint mill, 1 fulling mill.

The Rev. James Scott died on 28th February 1804, in the 30th year of his ministry. He was succeeded by the Rev. George Addison, who was translated 6th August 1817 to Liff and Benvie. His successor was the Rev. George Winehouse of Clova, who was presented to the living by Walter, Earl of Airlie. He died in London 28th June 1851, aged about 70, in the 38th year of his ministry. The last minister appointed by patronage was the Rev. Hugh Lyell, who died in 1878, after a ministry of 33 years.

In 1881 the interior of the church was entirely modernised, and rendered more seemly and comfortable for divine service, through the liberality of the heritors.

Within the churchyard there still remain a few tombstones of the seventeenth and eighteenth centuries; but these apparently have only been spared from the fact that they were too massive to remove easily.

Heir lyes ane godly and vertuous man, lames Christie of Balbeuchlie, who departed ye 20 of Decern. 1651, and his age 97:
Qui bene vivit bene morietur (who lives well will die well).
Dulce fuit quondam mihi vivere non quia vixi
Sed quoniam ut vivam tunc moriturus eram.
Once it vas svet to me to leive, not that I leived, but I leived to die.

Some of the poetical inscriptions upon the old monuments are of a very quaint and pathetic character.

The night of death is sveet Unto beleivers why 1 It doth the just inveet Into eternety.
By God's commission Death has called

These virtuous souls away; Their body sleeps in Christ, but shall
Awake at the last day.
Death is the debt to nature due, I've paid that debt, and so must you.
Here lowly lys a much regreted wife, Dear to the husband as his vital life.
Behold how numerous and how thick
The graves about you lye, On this reflect, O mortal man,
That shortly thou must die.
ANGUS PARISH. f
What is man's life that swifter far
Than weaver's shuttle flies, To troubles born, he weeps awhile,
And mourns, sighs, groans, then dies. Pray, then, improve thy precious hours,
Repent, do not delay, For who can promise on the next
That is in health to-day.
Time ripens mortals for the grave, And death soon cuts them down;
But they that Jesus Christ receives, Shall live and wear a crown.
Tho' in the grave their bodies ly,
Now sleeping in the dust, We hope, thro' Christ, they'll rise again,
And mingle with the blest.
All mortal bodies from the dust
At first did spring and rise, To it again descend they must
No mortal lives but dies.

Avchterhows, 1651. Remember man, as Thov goes by, As Thov art nov, so ones was I; AS I am Nov, so Thov most bee; Remember, man, that Thov most die. 0 Crovel Death, Thou cvts the Breth And taks the lyif avay.

James Nikol, 1654.

Heir lyes ane godlie and verteous man, Iohn ire, svmtirae- hvsband to Christian Young, in Bvrnside of Auchterhous, who departed. day of August 1669, and of his age 33. I. U. C. Y.

Heir lyes David Cuthbert, and Elizabeth Robertson, his Spous, indwellers in Pittulpie. He departed the. day of April 1689, of age G8. Shoe depairted 20 November 1689, of age 60. Also Euphane Allerdice, Spous to Iames Cuthbert, in Scotstoun. Shoe depairted the 11 January 1692, of age 56.

Here lyes ane godly and virtuous honest man, James JSTickle, in Kirktoun of Auchterhouse, and Janet Low, his wyfe. He depairted upon 1 day of Apryl, in the yeare of God 1682, and of his age 80 years.

Eecaus my soule in grave to dwell
Shall not be left by the; And with thy lykness when I wake I satisfied shall be.
An honest, quiet, and upright man,
Resolved to death here lys; His soul, by faith in Jesus' blood,
Now soars above the skys. When Christ the Lord in glory comes
To his compleat salvation, His dust shall quicken into life
At the great consummation.

James Stewart, Cotton of Auchterhous, hd. of Janet Mearns, d. 1780, a. 62.

In foreign lands, where men with war engage, He was sarvising at maney a bloody saige, And was preserved unhurt, ye gathered to his rest In frood old ao; e who trust in God is blist.

James Petrie and Margaret Anderson. He died in 1717, aged 61. She in 1734, aged 70.

This man and wife, during their life,
Each one in their vocation, Lived in peace, and now they cease
From toil and all vexation.

111 the higher districts of the parish, which have been comparatively free from agricultural encroachments, there are to be found many traces of the existence of stone tumuli or cairns those rude and primitive structures which marked the burial-places of the aboriginal tribes. In that dim and distant period prior to Roman civilisation, veneration and affection for the dead were expressed by the erection of such massive structures. Those conically-shaped were the favourite Celtic monuments, and from the immense amount of material employed in their erection, they must have entailed enormous labour. The sepulchral chamber over which the great cairn was constructed consisted of rows of stones set on edge, upon which other slahs rested. Within the rude chamber thus formed the body of the Celtic warrior was placed, generally in a contracted position, with the knees drawn up to the breast. Beside the body were deposited urns and other relics, along with the weapons supposed to be necessary for future happy hunting-grounds. Those ancient structures in this locality have long since been demolished and spoiled of their interesting and valuable historic contents. As we wander over those hills and lonely muirs, we are apt to regard these relics of former times as worthless detritus. Still, if we are true to our humanity, Ave cannot forget that these were the tributes of affection from grateful hearts and willing hands in the far-off times. Xear the foot of Auchterhouse Hill there is still to be seen, in a wonderful state of preservation, a very fine example of an ancient Cromlech. These Cromlechs or Druidical altars, as some have erroneously termed them, were the most important and valuable sepulchral monuments of the primitive races, and are rarely to be found. Although they are only rudimentary and symbolic forms of architecture, still, from an archaeological standpoint, they are of great interest. They were only erected in honour of some high personage, such as the chief of a tribe, and were regarded with great veneration, and within comparatively re cent times the stones of which they were constructed were viewed as sacred by the superstitious. They were erected on commanding positions, and formed of several large unhewn monoliths. These were so arranged as to form a chamher for the reception of the body of the chief, which was, placed in the usual contracted position, accompanied with urns and weapons, besides other still more valuable deposits. This Cromlech appears to have been encircled with a ring of stones, popularly but erroneously known as Druidical circles.

About the beginning of the present century, when a worthy old parishioner was having some repairs carried out upon his house, he removed a few of the lar. se stones with the intention of having them built into the walls. Throughout the night, however, an eerie feeling came over him, his conscience was on fire, he could get no rest. Accordingly begot out of bed, yoked his horse into the cart, and like a sensible man replaced the sacred stones where he found them, went home, and thereafter slept the sleep of the righteous.

South of the Tcmplclands another group of those mysterious circular stone relics of pagan times at one time stood, and was also held in much regard, and recognised as an ancient place of worship. This group, however, unfortunately was demolished during excavations for railway purposes. In the course of agricultural operations upon the farms of Leoch and Templeton numerous cists have been discovered. According to the primitive custom, these were rudely constructed of unhewn slabs, and contained the ashes of the dead. Many were discovered in regular rows, and at equal distances apart. From their number it is quite reasonable to conclude that this locality was the scene of frequent conflicts for supremacy between rival tribes in distant times, and that those slain were buried where they fell.

For many long years savage warfare prevailed between the Picts and Scots for supremacy. In the ninth century a great battle was fought between these two powerful rivals over the stretch of country between the Law of Dundee and this same district, the Picts being under the command of Brude, and the Scots under Alpin. This battle, known as the Battle of

Pitalpiu, terminated in the total defeat of the Scots. Alpin, their leader, was taken prisoner, beheaded on the spot, and his head borne in triumph to Abernethy, then the Pictish capital.

The root " pit," which occurs in names in the locality and in the immediate neighbourhood, such as Pitpointie, Pitnappie, Pitermo, Pitalpin, Pitempton, and which is peculiar to Pictland, seems to imply that this district formed at one time a portion of the Pictish settlements.

On the farm of Leoch, a strong plate formed of a conglomerated mass of vitrified stones, was struck by the plough, and when cleared it was discovered to be of circular shape, and twelve feet in diameter. Upon the plate there lay a quantity of decomposed bones, two inches thick, covered with ashes of burnt wood. In the neighbourhood, urns, necklaces, rings, bronze pins, and ornaments of shale have been discovered in ancient places of burial. On the top of Auchterhouse Hill there are still to be seen distinct traces of one of those circular forts frequently to be met with on the tops of our Scottish hills. They were generally constructed upon conspicuous conical hills overlooking a wide, extent of country, and many of them were of great strength. They were coronet-shaped, and consisted of several rings of loose stones, with trenches and carefully-guarded approaches. The one on this hill must have enclosed fully two acres of ground, with its succession of walls, ramparts, and other modes of defence. Traces of another primitive hill fort are distinctly to be seen on the summit of West Mains Hill. The site is a spacious and commanding one, and must also have formed an excellent point for military reconnoitring purposes in the subsequent days of the Clan invasions, as it is in direct line with that part of Strathmore by which an army might contemplate an attack upon Dundee by the pass of Newtyle. It not only commands a fine view of the Grampians, but has an uninterrupted outlook toward the Law of Dundee, at one time an important point of observation and signal station during the wars in which the district was involved.

Two of these remarkably interesting dwellings, called weems, have been discovered, one of them not far from the church, and the other near the mansion-house. In the former the space between the walls and the covering was full of rich mould, in which were found ashes of burnt wood, bones, and other deposits, formed by the refuse of ancient repasts. In the latter were found bones, several ancient querns or handmills (14 inches in diameter), a bronze ring of primitive workmanship, and the bones of animals. In the immediate neighbourhood two similar subterranean dwellings were also discovered. One of these contained apartments constructed entirely of large flat stones. In these recesses were found wood ashes, several fragments of large stone vessels, and a quern. The other was simply a vault, in which were found a large stone vessel, and a stone celt or hatchet. These weems were occupied by the primitive races, who existed mainly by hunting. They were the rude dwellings of a barbarous age the age of flint flakes, stone weapons and utensils. These strange habitations were generally located in knolls, and constructed in groups. The natural rock formed the floor of those retreats. The walls were made of stone, while the roof was formed by a gradual narrowing and overlapping of the stones. Within, there was generally a large apartment, from which diverged many other smaller recesses. The whole structure was carefully covered with layers of turf or peat, so that there was very little indication of it being a human habitation. The amount of physical labour expended upon these artificial dwellings must have been very great, and the skill and architectural ingenuity displayed are amazing for the age. Among their contents there are generally found stone celts and ancient querns. In construction these querns are exceedingly simple. They consist of two thin circular flat stones, the upper one of which is pierced in the centre, and revolves in a wooden pin inserted in the under one. These were used as domestic hand-mills, and querns of almost similar construction are still in use in some remote parts of the Hebrides. Occasionally within recent years stone coffins have been discovered in the neighbourhood of Greenford, the Old Toll, Bonniton, and Dronley. These stone coffins, however, cannot be reckoned in all cases prehistoric; because this mode of burial was not unusual in Highland districts in Romish times.

Sculptured Stone from Wallace Tower.
Abbot of Arbroath. 28.
Aberdeen Assembly. 74.
Act of Classes. 108, 125.
Act against Quakers. 147.
Act of Security. 149.
Act against Smuggling. 151.
Addison, Rev. George. 155.
Adultery. 84, 90, 94.
Agents of Jacobite Party. 140.
Airlie Castle. 44.
Airlie, Countess of. 51.
Airlie Family. 43-51, 89.
Airlie, Laird of. 26.
Airlie Lands. 49.
Aisle, Ramsay. 13, 76.

Albany, Duke of. 27.
Ale Houses kept by Clergy. 71, 91.
Ale Houses. 94, 109, 125.
Altars. 69.
Anglo-Normans. 2.
Anglo-Saxons. 2.
Angus, Earls of. 6.
Angus, Men of. 6.
Angus, Sheriff of. 2.
Animals, Filthy. 64.
Arbroath, Battle of. 25.
Archbishops and Bishops. 130, 133, 135.
Archery. 23.
Ardchattan. 4.
Argyll, Marquis. 36, 44, 48, 78, 80, 92. 97, 99, 129. Arms of Buchan. 40. Armies and Fleets, Success of. 142. Auchindown. 31. Auchinleck, Rev. James. 126. Auchterhouse Estates. 50. Auchterhouse visited by Wallace. 11. Auchterhouse Castle taken by King
Edward. 13. Auchterhouse, Lord. 27. Auchtertyre Hill. 82. Auldearn, Battle of. 79. Authority of Scriptures. 71. Ave Maria. 66, 69.

Badenoch, Wolf of. 21.
Badges in use. 93.
Bagimont's Roll. 62.
Baillie, General. 80,
Bairns Greetin'. 81.
Banishment. 72, 83, 84, 129.
Banning. 121.
Bannockburn. 14,
Baptism. 64, 94, 128.
Baptistries. 64.
Bareheaded in Marketplace. 84.
Barrel for Communion Wine. 142.
Battle of Pitalpin. 160.
Beadles. 80, 88, 94, 100, 124, 135
Begging. 72, 73, 93, 144.
Bell-house Disturbance. 136.
Berwick. 2, 9.
Bible. 71, 72.
Bier, Parish. 94.
Bird-nesting. 133.
Birnam Wood. 11.
Bisset's Death. 12.
Bisset, Rev. Andrew. 145.
Black Agnes. 15.
Black Earnside. 12.

Bonniton Lands. 28, 29.
Books. 03.
Book of Constitutions. 71.
Book of Ordination. 76.
Bow Practice. 23.
Bow Butts. 23.
Box Empty. 93.
Boyd, Lord. 7, 9.
Boyne Water. 142.
Branks. 81, 83.
Bread and Water. 84, 129.
Brechin. 11, 31, 93.
Brecking Maliguants' Teith. 102.
Briggant Story. 69.
Brods. 141.
Bronze Pins Discovered. 161.
Buchan, Countess. 130, 131, 132.
Buchan (5th Earl). 32.
Do. (6th Earl). 32, 33, 34, 36.
Do. (7th Earl). 36, 37, 98, 108.
Do. (8th Earl). 40. Buckingham, Duke of. 33. Burgundy at Communions. 143.
Burials. 94.
   Cairns. 159.
   Campbell, Rev. James. 130, 131 32.
   Cannibalism. 69.
   Canons of Church. 62, 68.
   Canons, Secular. 66.
   Carnwath, Earl of. 41.
   Carrickfergus, Battle of. 15.
   Catechizing. 105.
   Catechisms. 101.
   Cattle Pasturing. 63.
   Cavalry Regiments. 82.
   Celibate State. 62.
   Celts (Stone). 162.
   Chalices. 69.
   Change Houses. 142.
   Chapels. 61.
   Chapin Aill. 86.
   Chaplainries. 65.
   Charles I. 33, 36, 78, 79.
   Charles, Prince. 33, 36, 114.
   Charmers. 88, 103, 122, 123.
   Cheek Burning. 72.
   Chivalry, Days of. 17.

Choristers. 66.
Christian, Countess of Buchan. 29-31
Christian Burial. 64.
Church of Auchterhouse. 32, 36.
Churches. 63, 67, 70.
Churchyards. 64.
Circular Stone. Relics. 160.
Cists. 160.
Civil "War. 70, 72.
Claret at Communions. 142.
Clatto Moor. 6.
Claverhouse. 49, 138.
Clova. 37.
Coffinings. 144.
Colkitto. 89.

Collecting Ladles. 141. Collegiate Churches. 66. Corn for Beadle. 150. Common Enemy. 110. Common Heid, A. 130. Communion (Crowds at). 149. Do. Elements. 125, Do. Sunday. 133, 134. Do. Cups. 60. Confession. 64. Confession of Faith. 101, 140. Consiguation Money. 134. Conspirators. 65. Convention of Estates. 138. Corruption of Clemy. 68. Cortachy Castle. 37, 40, 51. Cospatrick. 8. Coupar Angus. 59, 90. Court of High Commission. 76. Covenanters. 113, 125. Covers of Fonts. 75. Crawford, Earl of. 25. Crawford, Master of. 26. Creepies. 72. Cromlech, A. 159. Cromwell. 36, 49, 77, 99, 113. Cruiked Folk. 72. Cullen, Collection for People of. 88. Culloden, Battle of. 50, 51. Cursing. 85, 121, 130, 144. Cutting Ears. 72.

Dalhousie Family. 1. Dancing. 64. Daskes. 100,136.

Defence of Protestant Religion. 142. Deliverance froiu, Pretender. 150. Dials. 76.

Diocesan Episcopacy. 74. Directory for Worship. 101. Disorderly Scenes. 137. Distressed Gentlemen. 144. Disturbance in Church. 129. Dogs in Church. 81. Doites. 140.

Douglas Family. 16, 17, 19. Do. Lochleven. 29.
Douglas, Sir George. 32.
Do. Lady. 29.
Do. Marie. 32, 35, 36.
Do. Sir Robert. 30, 31.
Do. Sir William. 32.

Do. Mr Robert. 108. Douking. 84. Drains of Fonts. 76. Dress of Clergy. 73. Dronlaw Lauds. 58. Druidical Altars. 159. Drum, Lady. 105. Drunkenness. 85, 130, 142, 144. Drybreasted Ministers. 122. Drying Clothes. 100. Dudhope Castle. 37. Dudhope, Lord. 37, 98. Dunbar, Battle of. 117, 118. Dunbar, Castle of. 7, 11, 15. Duncan Family. 60. Dundalk, Storming of. 15. Dundee Castle. 5, 6. Dundee, Storming of. 37, 77, 80, 90, 117. Dunkeld. 5.

Dunkeld Diocese. 61, 136. Dunnottar Castle. 6. Dutch Coinage. 141. Dutch Fleet. 132.

Eagle, Bearing the. 2. Ear Burning. 73. Eassie. 24, 65. Edinburgh Castle. 15. Edward I."s Invasion. 2, 10. Education. 95. Elders. 94, 121, 144. Elders' Quarters.

134. Engagement, Unlawful. 36, 96, 97. Episcopacy. 73, 78, 129. Episcopacy Ended. 146. Erskine, David. 40. Erskine, Lady Elizabeth. 38. Examination. 101, 106, 123. Excisemen. 153. Excommunication. 86, 87. Expectants. 102.
Fallawsmill. 6.
Fallins: in Love with Christ. 122.
Falkirk, Battle of. 10.
Fast-Day. 82, 87.
Fasts. 87, 107, 132.
Feastings. 144.
Fenton, Margaret de. 24.
Fenton, William de. 28.
Festivals. 68.
Fights for the Ankers. 153.
Fighting in Church. 100, 128.
Findhaven. 42, 43.
Fines. 83, 91, 94.
Flag of Covenanters. 82.
Fleeing to Churches. 64.
Fletcher's Description of Times. 144.
Flyting. 83, 90, 112.
Fonts. 63, 64, 75. Football. 23. Fornication. 94, 131. Forthour Castle. 44, 105. Forts (Circular). 161. Fraser, Mr Thomas. 145-6. French Protestants. 138. Free Fights. 101. Funeralls, True. 38, 60. Funerals. 94.
Galfridus, Bishop. 61.
Glack of Newtyle. 70.
Glamis Castle. 4.
Glassin Window. 123.
Glencune. 21.
Gothic Architecture. 66.
Graham, Sir John de. 5, 7, 9, 10.
Graham's Knowe. 82.
Gray, Sir Ralph. 8.
Hamilton, Duke of. 36, 96, 97. Hangings. 72, 73. Hanoverian Succession. 42. Harlaw, Battle of. 21, 66. Hawtliornden Caves. 16. Hays of Brrol. 58. Hay, Sir Gilbert de. 58, 59.
Do. Sir John de. 58.
Do. Sir Nicholas. 58.
Do. Mr Robert. 60.
Do. Sir William. 60. Heads Shaved. 84. Henry of Lancaster. 17. Heretics. 72. Hermitage Castle. 18. Highlands and Islands. 99. Highland Youths. 99. Highway Robbers. 65. Highland Host. 49. Hiiing-Out System. 73. Honorius II., Pope, Bull of. 63. Humiliation. 83, 88, 112. Huntly, Marquis of. 26, 78, 92. Hwuchtyruus, William de. 2.
Impotent Folk. 72. Imprisonment. 84, 128. Incantations. 123. Incumbents, Prelatic. 133, 139. Indulgences. 136. Infamous, The. 103. Inns. 62, Inscriptions.

156. Intimation of Roups. 150. Intolerance. 147. Inverlochy. 90. Inverness. 109. Irish Language. 145. Irish Levies. 80, 89. Irish Protestants. 138.
Jacobites. 139, 140. Jacobite Designs. 150. Jacobite hold of the Parish. 146. James, "Hearty." 26, 27. James II., King. 136. Joanna, Queen. 65. Johnstone, Rev. Patrick. 147, 150. Joined to Satan. 103. Jougs. 81, 83, 85, 128.
Keeping Order. 134. Kennedy, Bishop. 25, 67. Keillor Lands. 65. Killiecrankie, Battle of. 40. Kilsyth, Battle of. 45, 46. Kinneir, Rev. David. 73, 76. King's Birthday. 135. King's Safe Return to London. 143. Kneeling before Presbytery. 103.

Lady Well, The. 124.
Lanark, Earl of. 96, 98.
Lauderdale, Earl of. 96.
Leishing Bairns. 129.
Leslie, General. 48, 92, 97.
Leven, Earl of. 97.
Lining of Fonts. 75.
Lindsays. 25.
Lintrathen, Ogilvie of. 65, 6C.
Loch Leven Castle. 29.
Lords, Covenanting. 36.
Lord's Day Profanation. 85.
Lord of the Isles. 21.
"Lowse Lines." 102.
Lundie. 8.
Lyell, Rev. Hugh. 145.
Lyke wakes. 105.
Lyon of Brighton. 42.
Lyon, Hon. Patrick. 41, 42, 43, 145.
Magistrates of Dundee. 133.
Mains Parish. 70, 73.
Malignants. 100, 109, 113, 125, 126.
Manifesto of Scots Army. 79.
Manners, Lord. 16.
Manse, 63.
Manse Built. 150.
Mansion House. 38.
Mar, Countess of. 34, 35.
Mar, Family of. 32, 33, 58.
Mar, Earl of. 21, 33.
Marjory, Countess of Buchan. 38, 40, 131.
Marriages. 64, 86, 108, 124, 134.
Marriages, Clandestine. 64, 86.
Marston Moor, Battle of. 45.
Mary, Queeu of Scots. 30, 31.
Masses Celebrated. 66, 68, 69.
Maut Barn, Wallace's. 6.

Meigle Parish. 70.
Merchants, Scots. 34.
Methven (Paul). 68,
Minister's Relict. 144.
Moderator, Constant. 130.
Monasteries. 66, 69, 95.
Monastic Centres. 61.
Money from Army. 98.
Monk, General. 37.
Monks. 68.
Monoliths. 160.
Montrose, Marquis of. 38, 45, 46, 78, 81, 109, 111. Montrose Haven. 10. Moonlight Flitting. 103. Moray, Regent. 30. Mortcloth. 143. Morton, Governor. 10. Muck Spreading. 102. Mulct Paying. 142. Munro, General. 97.
Nailing by Lug. 72. Nailing to Trone. 72. National Covenant. 76, 90, 99. Navy, Royal, Success of. 132. Necklaces Found. 161. Newtyle Castle. 79. Nevay. 65. Norham Castle. 20. Notaries. 61.
Notar Scribe to Session. 106. Nuns. 68.
Oath, Form of in Episcopal Times. 133. Oath taken by Knights. 22. Oaths, Character of. 148. Oath of Purgation. 148. Ogilvie, Sir Alexander. 24, 26, 65.

Do. Helen. 47, 49.
Do. Lord. 45, 47, 48, 49, 50.
Do. Lady. 105.
Do. Margaret, 27, 29.
Do. Sir Patrick. 24.
Do. Sir Thomas. 46, 49, 89.
Do. Sir Walter. 20,21,24. Orange, William of. 138. Ostiarius. 80.
Papists. 72, 100, 137, 140.
Paroch Kirks. 67.
Peunie Stone Game. 133.
Penny Bridals. 105.
Perth, Five Articles of. 33.
Perth, Covenanters' Headquarters. 81.
Philiphaugh, Battle of. 47, 110.
Picts and Scots. 160.
Pillare, in the. 130, 132.
Pinkie, Battle of. 29.
Plague, Great. 132.
Plaids in Church. 81, 92.
Playing. 64.
Pluscarden. 48.
Poor Gentlemen. 144.
Pope, Letter to. 14, 59.
Porch of Church. 68.
Post-Reformation Times. 72.

Preaching (No). 82.
Prebendaries. 66.
Pre! atic Party. 140.
Prelates. 65.
Presbyterian Clergy Attacked by Mobs. 150. Presbyterianism. 71, 74. Presbytery, Dundee. 102, 103, 133. Presbyterian Parity. 73. Preservation of King's Person. 143. Preston, Battle of. 36, 97. Prestonpans, Battle of. 50. Pretender, The. 41, 42. Priests, Education of. 61,63. Prisoner, Collection for. 125. Privy Council. 129. Proclamations. 135. Proclamation of Banns. 64, 106. Profane Gaird. 119. Promiscuous Dancing. 105. Protesters. 78, 83, 108,125. Provincial Councils. 62 Provostry. 66. Psalm Book. 71. Pulpit, Before the. 112 Pulpit Recess. 143. Punishment. 135.

Querns. 162.

Raising the Devil. 126. Ramesie, Simundus de. 2.
Do. William de. 2. Ramsay Family. 1.
Do. Sir Alexander. 14-18.
Do. Sir John. 4-13.
Do. Sir Malcolm. 20.
Do. Marjory. 14.
Do. Matilda. 28.
Do. Sir Robert. 20.
Do. Sir William. 20. Rebels. 109. Reconciliation. 93. Records of Victories. 154. Rectors, Parish. 62. Reformation. 69, 70. Religious Houses. 67. Resolutioners. 78, 108, 125. Revival of Puritan Discipline. 147. Revocation of Edict of Nantes. 138. Revolution. 137. Revolution Settlement. 138, 139. Robertson, Rev. John (I.). 77.
Do. do. (II.). 133.
Rings Discovered. 161. Rioting. 150. Roslin Muir. 8. Rothes, Earl of. 33, 34. Roxburgh Castle. 8, 17. Royal Authority. 139. Ruthven. 10, 12, 14.

Sabbath Observance. 91, 128.
Sacraments, Receiving of. 64.
Sackcloth. 81, 90, 123.
Salisbury, Earl of. 15.
Salmond Fishing. 135.
Saturday Preparation. 82.
Scandalizing Royal Family. 137.
School, Building of. 95, 96, 112.
Schismatic, The. 65.
Scolding. 112.
Scott, Rev. James. 150, 155.
Scourging. 73.
Seaforth, Earl. 86.
Searching Ale Houses. 94, 109, 125
Searching Houses. 72.
Seaton. 10.
Sectarian Army. 112, 114.

Securitie. 113.
Seik Folk. 72.
Service Book. 76.
Shale Ornaments Found.
Shearing on Sabbath Day
Sheriff of Angus. 2.
Sheriflmuir, Battle of. 42, 50, 150
Sir James the Rose. 52.
Siward, Sir John. 5.
Slandering. 83, 89.
Smoking. 144.
Smuggling Days. 151.
Snow Storm. 123.
Solemn League and Covenant 100, 102, 108, 129. Son of Perdition. 63. Sorcerers. 88. Spanish Court. 34. Spate, A. 71. Start, The. 37. States Provinces. 132. St Andrews Castle. 47.
Do. College. 63. St Johnstone. 5, 8, 11,12. St Mary's. 65. Stick with Cleek. 81. Stipend. 63. Stirling, Battle of. 7. Stocks. 91, 128. Stools in Church. 92, 100. Stool of Repentance. 88, 90, 123. Stone Coffins Found. 163. Stone Vessels Found. 162. Strathmartine Parish. 70, 73. Strathmore, Descent upon. 79.
Do. Earl. 146.
Do. Family. 41, 42, 60.
Strictness of Times. 148. Striking. 93.
Superstitious Dread of Cromlech. 160. Supplementary Act. 83. Surgical Operation. 151. Surrey, Earl of. 6. Swearing. 85, 128.
Takinnes Worn. Tar Brush. 81.
Tartan, Wearing of. 62.
Taverns. 85, 91.
Tealing Parish. 70, 73.
Templars, Knight. 60.
Templelands. 60.
Tent for Refreshments in Churchyard. 149.
Testimonials. 106, 148.
Thack for Kirk. 68.
Thanksgivings. 92, 110,112.
Threshing Corn. 101, 104.
Tickets. 134.
Tithes. 63, 65.
Tombstones. 156 9.
Tonsure, Wearing the. 62.
Tower, Wallace. 13.
Treaty of Union. 149.
Troopers from Parish. 36.
Troopers Employed for Suppression of

Smuggling. 153. Tulzing. 142. Tumuli. 159. Turks, Victims of. 125. Turners. 141.

Tyndale's New Testament. 68. Tyrie, Rev. Alex. 70, 73.

Ulster Over-run. 138. Unlawful Engagement. Urns. 161. 36, 96, 97, 109.

Vagabonds. 72, 93. Vagabond Schollers. 73. Vault for Burial. 76. Vessels, Sacred. 63. Vestments. 63, 69. Vicarage, The. 61, 62. Vicars. 63.

Vicci de Benimundus. 61. Victory in Ireland. 142. Violators of Churches. 65.

Wakes. 144.

Wallace, Sir William. 3-13.

Warning People. 81, 105, 123.

Water for Baptism. 64.

Waukening Sleepers. 81.

Weak Folk. 72.

Wedderburns, The. 68.

Weekly Catechizing. 101.

Weekly Lecture Day. 86.

Weems. 162.

Wells, Sacred. 124.

Wemyss, Rev. William. 78.

Whisky Smuggled. 152.

Wills, Making. 65.

Wine Cellar. 143.

Winehouse, Rev. George. 155.

Winning of a Living. 72.

Wishart. 68.

Witches. 88, 90, 103, 104, 122, 124, 133.

Wood Sales. 150.

Worm of Smuggler's Still. 154.

Worthless Incumbents. 140.

University of Toronto Library
REMOVE
CARD
FROM
THIS
POCKET
Acme Library Card Pocket LOWE-MARTIN CO. Limited